The Terrorism Survival Guide

The Terrorism Survival Guide

201 Travel Tips on How Not to Become a Victim

Andy Lightbody

FOREWORD BY DON MANN

Skyhorse Publishing

Skyhorse Publishing books may be purchased in bulk at special discounts for sales promotion, corporate gifts, fund-raising, or educational purposes. Special editions can also be created to specifications. For details, contact the Special Sales Department, Skyhorse Publishing, 307 West 36th Street, 11th Floor, New York, NY 10018 or info@skyhorsepublishing.com.

Skyhorse® and Skyhorse Publishing® are registered trademarks of Skyhorse Publishing, Inc.®, a Delaware corporation.

Visit our website at www.skyhorsepublishing.com.

10 9 8 7 6 5 4 3 2 1

Library of Congress Cataloging-in-Publication Data is available on file.

Cover design by Rain Saukas
Cover photo credit iStock

Print ISBN: 978-1-5107-1490-8
Ebook ISBN: 978-1-5107-1491-5

Printed in the United States of America

Contents

Foreword

Although the United States and many countries throughout the world have taken the threat of terrorism very seriously, since the late 1970s terrorism is at an all-time high, making travel abroad even more dangerous. The days of carefree travel have unfortunately come to an end.

Andy Lightbody's *The Terrorism Survival Guide* is an absolute must-read for anyone who travels abroad! This quick reference for the business traveler or for those who travel for pleasure is filled with vital need-to-know information on how to travel more safely in today's world.

Terrorism and crime against travelers abroad is on the rise. Travelers need to be careful when selecting travel destinations and more observant of their surroundings when traveling.

The State Department often puts out warnings such as this:

As terrorist attacks, political upheaval, and violence often take place without any warning, U.S. citizens are strongly encouraged to maintain a high level of vigilance and take appropriate steps to increase their security awareness when traveling.

In multiple regions, terrorists, guerrilla groups, and criminals seek to kidnap U.S. citizens to finance their operations or for political purposes. In the wake of well-publicized attacks against commercial aircraft in Egypt by ISIS and Somalia by al-Shabaab, the Department remains concerned that terrorists could again seek to down aircraft using concealed explosives or hijack commercial flights.

In addition to concerns stemming from terrorism, travelers should be alert to the possibility of political unrest, violence, demonstrations, and criminal activities when traveling.

Terrorists often attack "soft targets," places that tourists often frequent, such as airports, train and bus terminals, hotels, resorts, clubs, restaurants, sporting events, political demonstrations, holiday celebrations, places of worship, schools, parks, shopping malls, and markets.

As a traveler, you must understand that terrorist groups—along with their associates and those inspired by such organizations—are intent on attacking U.S. citizens wherever they are, sometimes with unexpected methods. They are increasingly using less sophisticated weapons, including knives, pistols, and motor vehicles, to keep the element of surprise.

We must all be cognizant of the fact that any one of us at any time could become a victim of an attack. Although we will never be 100 percent safe when traveling abroad, we can greatly reduce the risk by being prepared.

In *The Terrorism Survival Guide*, Andy Lightbody has conducted extensive research on the topics of terrorism, violent crimes, and traveling more safely abroad. He masterfully outlines simple security precautions that when properly conducted will make you, your family, your friends, and your business associates much safer when traveling abroad.

These days there are so many attacks that many find it overwhelming to keep current on this rising deadly threat. There is terror across Europe, there is terror across the world, and many analysts believe the worst is yet to come.

Back in November 2015, there was the Russian jet filled with innocent travelers and a bomb planted on it that killed all 224 on board. ISIS proudly claimed responsibility. "Find your black boxes and analyze them, give U.S. the results of your investigation and the depth of your expertise and prove we didn't do it or how it was downed. Die with your rage. We are the ones with God's blessing who brought it down. And God willing, one day we will reveal how, at the time we desire."

Also that same month, 130 people were killed in a series of terror attacks in Paris at "everyday" sites—the sports stadium, the busy streets, a popular restaurant/bar, and a concert hall. The attackers, armed with assault rifles and explosives, specifically targeted locations often frequented by tourists.

And then there was the Mali attack where heavily armed terrorists indiscriminately shot at travelers at the hotel, killing twenty-one innocent people. One of the victims stated: "These people started shooting. They were shooting at everybody without asking a single question. They were shooting at anything that moved." Dozens of innocent people were trapped in the building for hours not knowing if they would survive this brutal attack.

The trend to attack travelers, businesses, and government institutions is only increasing and the trend toward more horrific and violent attacks has increased as well.

Major sites like Rockefeller Center and Times Square in New York City have become potential targets. ISIS released a threatening video that featured footage of Times Square as a target.

In the last decade, there have been close to nine hundred attacks against airlines, charter flights, general aviation, and airports. Factor in attacks at hotels, targeted businesses, embassies, military bases, and countless innocent civilians, and the growing numbers are most distressing.

Despite our efforts in fighting terrorism, it is a horrific fact that the number of terrorist attacks worldwide has quadrupled since September 11, 2001 and twenty-three countries recorded their highest number of deaths from terrorism in 2015. Terrorists are now targeting private citizens in one of every three attacks, resulting in more than 40 percent of the fatalities. These are alarming statistics for the traveler.

As a result, approximately 10 percent of American travelers have canceled a trip in response to terror attacks, eliminating a potential $8.2 billion in travel spending in 2015 alone. The total economic impact of violence reached $13.6 trillion in 2015, or 13.3 percent of global GDP (gross domestic product).

Before traveling abroad, it is imperative that you understand the risks of your destination. Always remain alert to your surroundings. This does not mean you must be on edge or paranoid, just alert, vigilant, and observant.

Many have known for decades that when traveling abroad it is best to avoid the larger hotels preferred by the business travelers, to avoid large crowds wherever possible, to always have an evacuation plan, etcetera. However, there is a lot more to consider than these basic tips!

Andy Lightbody has done a brilliant job at focusing on the current threat and describing in an easy-to-read format just what any traveler can do to lessen the odds of being a victim to an attack.

As you read through this book, please keep in mind: it does not intend to turn anyone into a travel or terrorism expert nor was it written to scare people from traveling abroad. The sole intent of this book is to educate the reader, to factually state the current threat abroad, and to recommend ways to best protect you and the people you care about.

May you stay safe with your travels. As we say in the SEAL Teams, keep and use this guide as another "tool" in your toolbox. It is better to know it and not need it than to need it and not know it.

—Don Mann
SEAL Team SIX (retired)

INTRODUCTION

The age of carefree travel is over. The threats of criminal acts and of terrorism, both internationally and domestically, are a reality. *The Terrorism Survival Guide: 201 Travel Tips on How Not to Become a Victim* is an easy-to-read pocket guide with hundreds of tips that help take away the worry of business and vacation travels.

On average, there are over 93,000 daily flights originating from about 9,000 airports around the world. At any given time, this means there are between 8,000 and 13,000 planes in the air around the globe. According to the stats from The International Air Transport Association (IATA), over 3.5 billion people were expected to travel in 2016 via air transport (http://www.iata.org). That figure is expected to double to 7 billion travelers by 2034.

And *yes*, traveling in a commercial airliner still rates as being a lot safer than traveling by automobile. That, of course, is the good news. In 2016, the Aviation Safety Network (ASN) showed it was the second safest year on record to take a commercial airline flight. There were 19 fatal airliner accidents that resulted in 325 deaths. According to the ASN this translates to one fatal passenger flight per 3.2 million flights.

On September 11, 2001, terrorism came to the United States with the crashing of two terrorist-hijacked airliners into the World Trade Center in New York City. Killing nearly 3,000 people, Usama Bin Ladin and al-Qaida took responsibility. For all Americans, terrorism become a "domestic reality," and the days of "carefree travel" were over forever.

On the flip side, regardless of how you choose to travel for business or pleasure, the incidents of terrorism and crimes directed at travelers continues to increase. And while many, many terror attacks are not specifically targeting tourists, oftentimes an innocent traveler simply is in the wrong place at the wrong time and becomes a victim and a collateral causality.

In the 16 years since the infamous 9/11 attack, the worst year for terrorism was 2014 with 93 countries being victimized. The result of those 13,463 attacks resulted in 32,765 people being killed, and over 34,700 being injured. In addition, more than 9,400 people were kidnapped or taken hostage; many were victims of KFR (kidnapping for ransom) schemes. For 2015 (latest year of data available), terrorist attacks actually saw their first decline in numbers since 2010. However, it still resulted in 12,089 attacks, and the deaths of 29,376 innocent victims. Even with a statistical decline of around 10 percent, 2015 still rated as the second-worst year for terrorism and deaths since 9/11. All this, according to the Global Terrorism Database (GTD), which is an open-source database including information on terrorist events around the world. According to the GTD, there have been over 160,000 incidents from 1970 through 2016.

Their program, officially known as the National Consortium for the Study of Terrorism and Responses to Terrorism (START), is a University of Maryland–based research and education center comprised of an international network of scholars committed to the scientific study of the causes and human consequences of terrorism in the United States and around the world. The University of Maryland works in conjunction with the Department of Homeland Security Center of Excellence in their research and maintaining of their huge database (www.start.umd.edu).

Other interesting statistics from the 2015 GTD report are likely to make your skin crawl and reveal the severity of worldwide terrorism:

- Terrorism related to drug wars and cartel violence is not included in their lists.
- Private citizens were targeted in one out of every three terrorist attacks, and accounted for 43 percent of all deaths.
- In 2015 four groups were responsible for 74 percent of all deaths from terrorism: ISIS, Boko Haram, the Taliban, and al-Qaida.
- ISIS surpassed Boko Haram as the deadliest terrorist group in 2015. ISIS undertook attacks in 252 different cities in 2015 and was responsible for 6,141 deaths in the year.
- Twenty-three countries recorded their highest number of deaths from terrorism in 2015.
- There were 609 bombings by ISIS in 2015, and they were more deadly on average than previous years.
- Since 2006, 98 percent of all deaths from terrorism in the US have resulted from attacks carried out by lone actors.
- The global economic impact of terrorism reached $89.6 billion in 2015. The total economic impact of violence reached $13.6 trillion in 2015, or 13.3 percent of global GDP (gross domestic product).

Another alarming trend, this one for 2016, was the number of female terrorists, especially as suicide bombers. The Terrorism

While experts believe that the threat of terrorists being able to secure and detonate a nuclear bomb are low, they also warn that using a variety of nuclear waste materials can give radical activists the raw material to make a radiological "dirty bomb." It lacks the nuclear explosion and destructive power, but can be set off with conventional explosives and contaminate innocent civilians and areas with deadly radioactive contamination and fallout. Effects from such a terrorist device could contaminate an area for months or years. Photo courtesy of NCTC.

and Low Intensity Conflict Research Center at the Institute for National Security Studies (INSS), reports that forty-four suicide bombings were committed by women, with involvement of another seventy-seven females in eight countries. These *femme-fatale* terrorists are believed to have caused the death of approximately four hundred people in 2016.

Unfortunately, in the last ten years there have been over eight hundred attacks against airlines, charter flights, general aviation, and airports. Factor in attacks at hotels, targeted businesses, embassies, military bases, and countless innocent civilians—and the growing numbers are most distressing.

The trend to attack travelers, businesses, and government institutions is only increasing. While the overall number of attacks has continued to yo-yo up and down over the past decade, the trend toward more horrific and violent attacks has spiraled upward. Some of the most violent and world-headline-making attacks in the past few years include:

- the Fort Lauderdale airport shooting in the baggage claim area on January 6, 2017 that killed five people and left six injured from gunshots;

U.S. military bases and ports have long been top targets of international terrorist groups. The attack on the USS *Cole* off the Yemen coast in 2000 killed seventeen sailors and wounded thirty-nine others. Usama Bin Laden and al-Qaida were responsible for the attack. Photo courtesy of NCTC.

- the December 19, 2016 truck attack at the Christmas marketplace next to the Kaiser Wilhelm Memorial Church in Berlin, Germany, that left twelve people dead and fifty-six others injured;
- the nineteen-ton-truck rampage in Nice, France, on July 14, 2016, in which eight-five innocent men, women, and children were mowed down and killed while watching a Bastille Day fireworks celebration;
- a combined shooting/suicide bomber attack on June 28, 2016 at the Ataturk Airport in Istanbul, Turkey, that killed forty-five and injured 230 people;
- the horrific mass shooting/hate crime that killed fourteen parishioners and wounded three others at a Bible Study class at the Emanuel African Methodist Episcopal Church in downtown Charleston, SC. The gunman was a self-proclaimed white supremacist who was in hopes of starting a domestic race war;
- a total of forty-nine people were shot and killed, and another fifty-three were injured at a gay nightclub in Orlando, Florida, on June 12, 2016 when an American gunman said he was inspired by ISIS to attack;
- the March 22, 2016 airport and metro attack in Brussels (Zavantem airport and Maalbek Metro), in which travelers were attacked by suicide bombers. Thirty-two innocent people were

killed and over three hundred were wounded. An additional bomb was found during a search at the airport that luckily was not detonated, or casualties would have climbed even higher;

- a lone suicide bomber on March 19, 2016 attacked a popular tourist shopping area near the district governor's office in Istanbul, Turkey, killing five and injuring thirty-six;

- a suicide bomber attack near the Blue Mosque and the Hagia Sophia on January 12, 2016, in Istanbul, Turkey. The area was popular with tourists, and the blast killed thirteen people—all foreigners. Fourteen people, mostly tourists, were also wounded;

- the mass shooting attack in San Bernardino, California, on December 2, 2015 that left fourteen people killed and twenty-two others wounded by husband and wife self-proclaimed ISIS jihadists at a workplace Christmas party held at the Inland Regional Center;

- an extremely well-coordinated bombing and mass shooting attack in Paris and northern suburbs occurred in November 2015 when terrorists attacked cafés, restaurants, and even a large music concert hall. These attacks resulted in 130 dead and 368 wounded, many of whom were tourists;

- a Russian airliner (Metrojet Flight 9268), loaded with 224 tourists in October 2015 on a flight from the Egyptian resort city of Sharm el-Sheikh to St. Petersburg, Russia, is suspected of being brought down with a "soda can" bomb that had been hidden on board the plane. All 224 passengers and crew perished. Most all were foreign tourists;

- a dual attack by a naturalized American citizen who was also a "foreign-inspired terrorist," who opened fire on two military installations in Chattanooga, Tennessee, on July 16, 2015. After doing a drive-by shooting at a recruiting center, the terrorist continued his shooting attack at a U.S. Navy Reserve center. Six servicemen were killed and several others were wounded;

- the terrorist attacks in Paris in January 2015, which started

against the French newspaper *Charlie Hebdo*, killing eleven people and wounding eleven others in the building. After leaving, the terrorists killed a French National Police officer. Follow-on attacks in the region killed an additional five people and wounded eleven more;

- the Boston Marathon bombing in April 2013 with two pressure-cooker bombs that detonated and killed three people and wounded over 260 others.

Unfortunately, the world will have likely been rocked by additional horrific attacks after this book was published. I beg you to not look at *The Terrorism Survival Guide: 201 Travel Tips on How Not to Become a Victim* as a book designed to scare you, your family, your friends or business associates. If you are afraid to travel and cancel your trips because of fears of being attacked, then the bad guys have won a battle against you with unwarranted fear, and the threat of intimidation!

Instead I urge you to use these tips, which are designed for *everyone*, as a way to increase your travel awareness as to where you go and how you travel, as well as being able to better protect yourself personally and ensure that you have a safer journey.

Not everyone will relate to or need all of these travel tips. Many will even seem rather simple, or just how you should exercise your

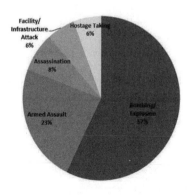

Far and away, the favorite weapons of most terrorist organizations are bombings and explosives.

common sense. The book also is not designed to make anyone into a travel or security expert. There are many higher-learning instruction classes and degrees to assist you on that path. Instead it should be used as a reference for many easy tips, information, and guidelines that anyone can use and incorporate into their travel plans.

The bottom line is, terrorism and crime against travelers is not going to go away. While we expect governments to provide security both here and abroad for our travels, it often comes down to learning, observing, and taking individual precautions to protect oneself, family, and friends.

The concerns and real dangers of crime and terrorism in today's world has made it a necessity for all travelers to be more observant and vigilant about everything from their travel destinations to what is going on around them at airports, hotels, resorts and with all aspects of traveling. Photo courtesy of U.S. Department of State.

My best wishes to all travelers in not being intimated, frightened, or scared needlessly!

Sincerely,
Andy Lightbody

1

TERRORISM DEFINITIONS

While domestic and international terrorism has been around for decades here in the United States and around the world, not only are there no worldwide answers on how to stop or even control these cowardly acts, there is not even one definition of "terrorism" that has gained universal acceptance! In spite of its insidious consequences to countless innocent victims, governments around the world (including the U.S. goverment) continue to look about as competent as if they were playing the old "whack-a-mole" game. Put it down in one place and it rears its ugly head somewhere else.

So, it is not too surprising that world governments, and even various agencies within the United States, all seem to have various definitions as to what "terrorism" is. The U.S. Department of Homeland Security, the FBI, the CIA, the U.S. Department of Defense, the U.S. Department of State, and even the United Nations, all have their own different definitions.

For the purpose of this book, probably the best "official" definition of terrorism is contained in Title 22 of the United States Code, Section 2656(d). That statute contains the following definitions:

The term "terrorism" means the premeditated, politically motivated violence perpetrated against noncombatant targets by subnational groups or clandestine agents, usually intended to influence an audience.

The term "international terrorism" means terrorism involving citizens or the territory of more than one country.

The term "terrorist group" means any group practicing, or that has significant subgroups that practice, international terrorism.

Generally speaking, the United States government has employed this definition of terrorism for statistical and analytical purposes since 1983.

And while an "official" definition of terrorism is a good starting point, it is likely not to mean very much to a traveler who becomes a victim of a criminal or terrorist act. In the course of dealing with, researching, reporting, and writing about terrorism, I've found that while we all know that any act of terrorism is a sinister and spineless act, the question remains: How do you break it down and get into the mind of what really motivates a terrorist? While no psychological profile is definitive, I've found the following to be virtually universal when trying to categorize the motives behind the dastardly deeds. One of the easiest ways to at least divide and label a terrorism act is to use the **Three Cs** method. In virtually all cases, the terrorist act can be put into category of being based as a **Criminal**, a **Crusader,** or a **Crazy:**

Criminal—usually motivated more by money or financial gain, rather than a deep-seated political or religious motivating factor. The United Nations Office on Drugs and Crimes said in one of its recent 2016 conferences that "growing evidence suggests that terrorist organizations are increasingly involved in kidnapping for ransom [KFR] for the purpose of obtaining political concessions as well as financial benefits, particularly in the Middle East and North Africa."

The payment of ransom money to terrorist groups is one of the sources of income that supports everything from their recruitment efforts and increased operational capabilities to being able to carry out terrorist attacks.

Some say that like the pirates that roamed the open seas back in the sixteenth and seventeenth centuries, these marauding money-hungry terrorists are looking more like well-paid mercenaries instead of political or religious zealots!

Unknowing and unwitting travelers are often easy and unsuspecting victims of KFR. It is so pronounced that al-Qaida leader Ayman al-Zawahiri has called for supporters worldwide to kidnap westerners as they could be exchanged for jailed jihadists or ransomed back to governments or families.

ISIS claims to have made over $45 million in 2014 through KFR and now has a special department dedicated to this activity!

Crusader—misguided and misdirected, the Crusader is an extreme true believer in a political or religious cause. Motivated to the point of committing acts that would lead to their own death, or simply by committing suicide, these "followers" are least likely to surrender, give up, or change their ideological or religious beliefs. The radical Muslim group ISIS, Usama Bin Laden, HAMAS suicide bombers, and others are well-known groups in this category.

Crazy—Most likely to be commonly-termed nuts, psychos, or mentally-deranged, these people perform acts of terror which are rarely based on rational thinking or thought. Often hearing voices or being directed and driven by uncontrollable urges, a Crazy terrorist is unpredictable in the acts, methods, or outcome of their attacks. Going into a school like Sandy Hook or a movie theater in Colorado or an airport in Fort Lauderdale and gunning down innocent people are but some of the incidents where the attacker was obviously unhinged.

Regardless of the motivation, all terrorists are extremely dangerous threats—that cannot be stressed or repeated often enough. And regardless of what may be actually going through the minds of these individuals or groups, the bottom line always has been and will be . . .

A terrorist is someone willing to give *your all* for his or her cause!

2

TRIP-PLANNING TIPS

Planning for a trip that is going to be a "new adventure" should begin well in advance of the day of departure. Plan ahead, do your homework, and know as much about where you are traveling as possible.

1. Adopt an anti-terror/anti-crime philosophy: Don't assume the typical "It-can't-happen-to-me" attitude. Travelers have long been top targets of terrorist and criminals. Each year, thousands of Americans and foreign travelers are victims of criminal acts and terrorism. The 9/11 attack in New York in 2001, as horrific as it was, is now ancient history! Attacks in Paris, Belgium, and throughout Europe, Asia, and Africa continue to grab world headlines. The nonprofit organization Investigative Project on Terrorism found that an average of nearly 30,000 people per year have been killed by terrorists since 2010. Back then, the terrorism death toll was 3,284. While the vast majority of the victims are not Americans, it still represents an 800 percent increase!

2. Be aware of terrorism and crime profiles of countries you plan to visit: With a little advance research, you'll know which countries are soft targets and do little to protect travelers or even their citizens from potential terrorist attacks. You'll learn that purse snatchers prowling on scooters are now so common in Italy that police give victims preprinted forms to fill in. Pickpockets are rife all over Western Europe, rental cars are top auto theft targets in Spain, your luggage is most likely to be pilfered on your journeys throughout Southeast Asia, and so on.

3. Learn the customs and the laws: Each year over 7,500 Americans are arrested in foreign countries—for drugs, illegal currency exchanges, custom violations, religious practices, etc. Some are arrested for crimes they did not know existed. Over 60 percent of all American arrests abroad are *not* drug-related. So, learn all the local customs that could be law violations—possessing pornographic magazines in China, chewing bubble gum in Singapore, wearing military clothing in Ghana, handing out a Bible in Saudi Arabia, etc. Contact the U.S. embassy in the country you are visiting or the State Department before you go to receive advisories along these lines.

4. Don't be an obvious visitor: This simple advice is often overlooked by many travelers. Many tourists are easy to spot. Plan to

Many countries have drug laws that are a lot harsher than those in the United States. Know before you go and use! In some states the use of cannabis (marijuana) is legal, however transporting it back home with you via vehicles or commercial airlines is not. Get caught taking even a small amount back home with you, and you will be arrested!

lower your profile, don't be obnoxious or snooty, and do pay heed to the old adage, "When in Rome, do as the Romans do."

5. Avoid the known hot spots: If terrorism—domestic or international—is high or uncontrolled in the area you are planning to visit, it might be best to avoid going there. If there is a high rate of criminal attacks and acts against visitors, find out before you go and plan to either develop security plans to protect yourself, or plan your trip for a later date.

6. Research your travel destination: Get on the Internet, and start reading about the area you plan on visiting. Start finding and reading—either online or at your newsstand or library—several of the local daily and weekly newspapers. They will provide you information from specific crime waves to unexpected tourist opportunities. For international travelers, this advance research can offer great insight into the political stability of the region.

7. Use the travel experts: Use of a veteran travel agent or travel club representative (AAA, AARP) costs the traveler no more than having to go through all the time-consuming booking arrangements by yourself. Booking through a reputable travel agent can not only eliminate problems, but can help ensure that everything will come together well. When booking a package tour, make sure that the tour operator belongs to the United States Tour Operators Association (USTOA). This organization's members are backed by a $1 million Travelers Assistance Program, an insurance policy that protects the traveler in the event the individual tour company folds. It is not a personal protection insurance group or policy. Check their members by calling 212-599-6599, Fax: 212-599-6744, or visit their website at www.ustoa.com.

8. Avoid travel fraud and scams before you go: The National Consumers League in Washington, DC, reports that travel fraud and scams cost American citizens over $40 billion annually, mostly in telemarketing schemes. Unfortunately, one out of seven of these rip-off schemes are travel-related, and are still perpetrated by using telephone telemarketers (46 percent of complaints) or through the Internet (32 percent of complaints). The bottom line is, *if the trip sounds too good to be true, it probably is.* If someone asks for your checking account or credit card number to secure your prize, it is likely to be a criminal who is going to rip you off! Over fourteen thousand illegal telephone sales are made daily to bilk unwise consumers. For information or to report an abuse, go to www.fraud.org or call 202-835-3323.

9. Be smart selecting a hotel: Small local hotels, motels, and bed-and-breakfast accommodations are rarely targeted by criminal gangs or terrorists. Domestically and abroad, the non-neon accommodations help tourists blend in with the local population.

10. Ask about security at flagship hotels: Often located near air-

Domestically or internationally, small non-flagship affiliated hotels and motels may not be as glamorous and opulent as the big chains, but they are often a lot more affordable and are not usually on the radar for criminal or terror attacks. Big-Box hotels are often snooty, while locally-owned guest accommodations are family friendly, and give you a better feel for where you are visiting.

ports and major metropolitan centers, the large luxury hotels have in the last twenty years been popular targets for everyone from criminal gangs to prostitution rings to terrorists looking to make tourists and business travelers victims of their attacks. If staying at a U.S.-associated major hotel, ask questions about security before you book your reservation and literally bet your life on their preparedness to handle the life-threatening situations. Ask about security in and around the hotel. Do they have security cameras throughout the hotel and the parking lots? Are the cameras actually monitored and recorded? Do they have any on-site security guards? Do you have to show your room key to security before approaching guest elevators?

Every year, tens of thousands of lawsuits are filed against U.S. hotels for negligent, lax, or nonexistent security. Jury awards back to the plaintiff have often been over $1 million.

11. Watch your clothing style: Avoid packing and wearing styles

Hotel lobbies at expensive "flagship" hotels are often targeted by terrorists and criminals for attacks on travelers. The scenery may be magnificent, but the security is often lacking. Once you have checked in, it is best to exit those areas as soon as possible. Meetings with friends, family, or clients in hotel lobbies, restaurants, or bars close to the entrance should be avoided.

that don't fit with the local area. The three-piece power suit can immediately identify you as a wealthy businessperson. Other clothing tip-offs include Hawaiian shirts, clothing with university or pro-team sports logos, camo patterns, cowboy boots and hats, flashy belt buckles, lots of jewelry, and expensive designer luggage, briefcases, or handbags.

12. Avoid military fashions in particular: Never travel with military-style clothing—khaki pants, camouflage shirts, berets, or even military patches, insignias, or boots. Often worn by young people, this clothing style can be easily misidentified by terrorists or criminals as someone who may have a military affiliation.

Always watch what you wear and how you dress. The best idea is to "blend in" with the people at your destination and not draw attention to yourself or that you are an American traveler. Lots of jewelry, expensive clothing, and furs should be locked in your checked luggage until you arrive at your destination and need them. These kind of hats should be left at home!

13. Avoid wearing jewelry: When traveling, it's best to carry your jewelry instead of wearing it. Wedding bands and rings are okay, but all the other flashy stuff can identify you as a wealthy traveler. Large gold chains, Rolex watches, heavy bracelets, and even fraternity or sorority rings need to be packed away in your carry-on luggage until you reach your destination where the jewelry can be brought out in an area and shown off accordingly and when appropriate.

14. Keep your hair and style simple: Very short crew cuts on men can mislead terrorists into thinking you are a member of the military. Shaved heads, wild hairstyles like Mohawks, or multi-colored dyed hair can identify you as a decadent to many terror groups. Keep the facial or body-piercings to a minimum or none at all.

15. Be savvy about organized tours: While there is a certain amount of truth in the saying "there is safety in numbers," medium to large tour groups on pre-planned, organized, and very structured tours can be prime targets for terrorists or criminal gangs. Avoid the tour groups that pick up just outside the major hotel door and advertise that a major tour group is being organized. Arrange the pick-up point for you and family members to be at the tour venue or other pre-arranged locations.

16. Research major regional events: If large events and celebrations are planned—such as military shows, national celebrations, or anniversaries—you may want to avoid these unless they're part of your original itinerary. Here in the United States, a quick call or web search to the local chamber of commerce or regional tourism office can give you a complete update on local activities and festivities. If you're traveling abroad, call the U.S. embassy or contact the nation's international consulate office to find out what major events are scheduled.

The insidious nature of a terrorist attack is that nobody knows where or when it will happen. Large gatherings, events, and celebrations are a favorite target for sneak attacks. At the Boston Marathon in 2013, two homemade "pressure cooker bombs" exploded within twelve seconds of each other about two hundred yards apart. Three people were killed and 264 were severely injured. Photo courtesy of NCTC.

17. Get your passport: As of January 1, 2008, the United States requires *all* U.S. citizens to have a valid passport in order to travel abroad—land, sea, or air. A passport is not required for travel by U.S. citizens to any territory or waters, continental or insular, subject to the jurisdiction of the United States (including Puerto Rico, Guam, American Samoa, and the U.S. Virgin Islands.) However, even crossing into border towns of Mexico or Canada does require a valid passport or passport card.

Make sure that yours is up to date and not close to expiring. Some countries require that your passport has a minimum of six months left (before expiring) to be valid for entry into their country. Some airlines will not allow you to board if this requirement is not met. Up-to-date information on passports and applications is available at the National Passport Information Center, on their website at www.travel.state.gov; telephone: 877-487-2778.

Travelers need to treat their passports like gold! They are now required for virtually all international travel by U.S. citizens, and remain a top target of criminals for theft. Allow yourself enough time to apply for your passport or your foreign travels are not going to happen. Also make sure that your existing passport is current and not going to expire while you are traveling! Photo courtesy of U.S. Department of State.

18. Passports vs. passport cards: Passports are valid for international travel by air, sea, or land. A passport card is valid *only* when entering the United States from Canada, Mexico, the Caribbean, and Bermuda at land border crossings or sea ports of entry. It is not valid for international travel by air. They are valid for ten years for adults, and five years for minors (under sixteen years old).

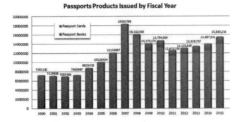

Passports for adults are valid for ten years. For minors/children that are under fifteen years of age, the passport is valid for five years. Expect that it usually takes four to six weeks to process your passport request paperwork, so plan accordingly!

19. Write contact numbers in your passport: It's a good practice to write down the names and telephone numbers of your family, friends, and office contacts to be called in the event of an emergency. Near the front of your passport is space that is reserved for this purpose. Also, put your blood type and any information regarding allergies, medications, or medical conditions on a piece of paper and tape it in your passport.

20. Visas are not passports but often needed in advance of travels: Depending on which country you are planning to visit, you may also need a visa. A visa is an official document issued by a foreign country that formally allows you to visit. Visas are attached to your passport and allow you to enter the foreign nation. A visa from a foreign country is not your passport! Look through the State Department's *Country Specific Information* (www.travel. state.gov/content/passports/en/country.com) for detailed information about your destination. You can research the entry and exit requirements, get more details about necessary documentation, and find out how to apply. You may be able to apply online, at that country's U.S. embassy or even at the airport in the country itself once you get there.

21. Consider a few low-tech security devices: A host of low-tech security devices are now on the market. Most of these devices can be purchased over-the-counter and require no special training or permits for personal safety. These items include hand-held "screamers/screechers," high-intensity flashlights, portable hotel security door jammers, key-chain batons, pepper-gas sprays, and even tear gas. Do keep in mind that transporting self-defense sprays with more than 2 percent of tear gas is prohibited in checked luggage (and, of course, all weapons are banned from carry-ons). Buy it when you arrive in your destination city and trash it before you get back to the airport for your return flight.

22. Consider high-tech security devices, too: Here is where you can literally enter the world of secret agents. If you consider yourself a mark for a possible terrorist or criminal attack, you can find new gear available to protect you, such as telephone debuggers, bulletproof clothing, emergency signaling and locator devices, tamperproof briefcases, portable door alarms or tripwire devices, anti-kidnap sprays, and a host of car protection devices that would make James Bond envious.

23. Take security training: If you are a high-risk target, a frequent traveler, or even a student planning on studying overseas, you may want to consider taking training classes in anti-crime or anti-terrorist procedures from reputable companies that specialize in training. Exploresecure (www.exploresecure.com), Safe Travel Solutions (www.safetravelsolutions.org), the Personal Safety Training Group (www.personalsafetygroup.com), IHS Training (www.ihs-training.com), and others provide everything from online video courses to corporate seminars.

24. Hire a security consultant: If you are in a high-risk category, such as a multi-nation globetrotter traveler for fun or business, you or your company may want to hire an outside security agency to assist in designing future travel plans. Not only can these firms provide up-to-the-minute information on crime and terror incidents, but they can also provide advance scouting, routing, and security checks of areas to be visited.

25. Get security reports: In the old days before 9/11, if you wanted to stay up to date on possible terrorism and crime incidents, you had to subscribe to newsletters that were produced by security companies, paying quite a bit for these updates. Today, you can simply use the resources of the U.S. State Department by going to www.travel.state.gov and get a full and complete detailed listing of all Travel Warnings and Travel Alerts from around the globe. You can also check the status of over 150 individual countries, as well as enroll in their Smart Traveler Enrollment Program (STEP) and receive country updates at no charge.

26. Make security plans: Does your company or corporation have a security plan in the event you become a victim of a criminal act or terrorist attack? If not, it's time to start one. Professional security consultant firms such as GlobalSecur (www.globalsecur.com), iJET (www.ijet.com), Pinkertons (www.pinkertons.com), and others can help.

27. Let everyone you trust know about your travel plans: Openly discuss your travel plans with people in your family, friends, and trusted associates. Oftentimes these people can be your additional "eyes and ears" to the area that you plan to visit. If there are additional security alerts and information about the area where you are traveling, it's nice to have a lot of people looking out for your welfare and best interests.

28. Leave behind a detailed itinerary: Leave a full and complete copy of your travel plans with your business associates, family, and friends. Make sure that everyone knows where you are going, how long you will be there, how you are traveling (airline, ship, ground transport), how they can contact you, and when you plan to return. Insist that nobody gives out this information to anyone but trusted business contacts, family members, or the properly identified authorities. If you change your travel plans, telephone or email these folks so that everyone knows about your updated travel plans. You might also want to include a secret word or phrase in them that will let everyone know that you are okay . . . or send up a *red flag*, alerting everyone that you are in trouble!

29. Make copies of tickets, passports, and credit cards: Make copies of all important documents you plan to travel with—this includes all airline or train tickets, passports, credit cards and ATM cards, hotel confirmations, traveler's check numbers, doctor's and dentist's telephone numbers, instructions on how to cancel credit cards (domestically or internationally), etc. Leave one copy with your office and a second set of papers with your family and friends. Take another set or two along with you in your checked luggage in the event these important papers are stolen.

30. Treat your airline tickets like cash: Nowadays, the majority of airlines issue electronic airline tickets rather than traditional paper airline tickets. They can't be lost or stolen, and if you lose your itinerary, go online and print a fresh copy.

However, some airlines in smaller foreign countries still use paper. If your airline tickets are lost or stolen, you are often going to have to pay a "continuation of travel fee," or buy new ones in order to complete your travels! All the airlines require passengers to fill out a Lost Ticket Form, and will then provide you a refund—in six weeks to four months! Make sure you have cash reserves or a credit card with a high enough financial limit to cover this contingency.

31. Photo IDs are now a must: Always travel with at least two photo identification pieces with you at all times. This will usually include a driver's license, passport, military ID card, etc. Airlines and cruise ships are not going to let you board their craft unless you can be positively identified. And here in the United States, *all* domestic airlines and the DHS are going to demand a photo ID beginning on January 22, 2018. According to the TSA and DHS, after that date you will not be permitted through the security checkpoint if you cannot provide an acceptable form of identification. A state-issued weapons permit or temporary driver's license is not an acceptable form of identification!

32. Take along extra photos of yourself: Citing national security, the U.S. State Department refuses to say how many U.S. passports are lost or stolen each year by American citizens. Considering that a valid U.S. passport is extremely valuable to anyone from criminals to terrorists, it is not too far to guess that many tens of thousands are lost or stolen each year. Based on lost and stolen passports reported by other countries as a comparison, odds are that at least one in every 1,500 American travelers is going to be stuck in some foreign country without documentation to return to the United States. If your passport is lost or stolen, having extra (identical to your passport) photos will speed the process of getting you a replacement.

33. Cash, checks, credit/ATM cards: If you are on a domestic flight in the US, there is no limit to the amount of cash that you can carry. If you are traveling internationally, the maximum amount is $10,000 in currency. In days gone by, the preferred way to travel with money was to use traveler's checks. Today, while still available with a few banks, they have pretty much gone the way of the dinosaur. Many foreign banks, hotels, etc., will no longer accept them, or if they do, be prepared for costly acceptance fees. Best advice is to use research the area of your travels and make sure that your bank-issued credit card or ATM card will be accepted. Major credit cards—Visa, MasterCard, and American Express—usually have no problems.

Companies such as Travelex Currency Services (www.travelex. com) can sell you a multi-currency Cash Passport. These travel money cards can be purchased before your travels and loaded with currencies from around the world, including Euros, British Pounds, Australian Dollars, Japanese Yen, Canadian Dollars, and Mexican Pesos.

34. Put your personal affairs in order: To ensure your family's financial security is taken care of in the event you become a victim of an accident, criminal act, or terrorist disaster, make sure your will or trust is up to date. Make sure you have specified who is going to have power of attorney, and that an estate executor has been specified.

35. Buy travel insurance: If you're a frequent domestic or international traveler, you know airline travel is about twenty-five times safer than driving your car. Still, adding additional life insurance either at the airport or by simply charging your airline flight to one of the major credit cards, can add nearly automatic additional coverage of $1 million or more. In the event of a catastrophic event, this additional coverage is virtually guaranteed. Companies like Travelex Insurance (www.travelexinsurance.com or 800-228-

9792), International Insurance Group (www.internationalpro.com or 888-467-4639), and Allianz Travel Insurance (www.allianztravelinsurance.com or 866-884-3556) can offer you quotes over the Internet or by calling.

36. Update your homeowner's and life insurance: Make sure you've got all the insurance you want and need. Some policies cover you for foreign property loss and injury—others do not. Most, but not all, cover you when traveling for business and vacation here in the United States. Many are extremely limited or virtually worthless for travel to foreign nations. Check your policies with your local insurance agent.

37. Call your doctor and dentist: Make sure all medical and dental records are up to date in the event of an airline crash, accident, or attack. These records will be needed by domestic or foreign emergency medical facilities in the event you become a victim of an accident, a medical emergency, or even a criminal attack on a national and worldwide basis.

38. Bring along medical notes: If you suffer from any sort of chronic condition, you'd be wise to invest in some sort of medical alert bracelet. With conditions such as diabetes, high blood pressure, heart problems, etc., it can be critical to your survival to let medical personnel know—especially if you can't talk for yourself. Even if you have only a short-term condition or are taking medication, it's important this information is written down and in your wallet or purse at all times.

39. Buy special medical insurance: As surprising as it may sound, some 6,000 American citizens die in overseas locations each year.

In addition, nearly 20,000 become ill or are injured and require hospitalization while traveling abroad. Insurance policies to cover everything from emergency medical coverage, translation and legal services, to medical evacuation flights back to the United States are available. Social Security's Medicare program *does not* provide for hospital or medical costs outside the United States.

Major insurance companies, as well as most major credit card companies, can offer short-, medium-, and long-term policies that can save you anywhere from $30,000 to $300,000 or more in emergency medical aid. MEDjet International, 800-356-2161 (www.medjet.com); Global Rescue, 800-381-9754 (www.globalrescue.com); and U.S. Air Ambulance, 800-633-5384 (www.usairambulance.net) offer worldwide air medical transport service with 24-hour-a-day assistance. Other corporations offering membership insurance policies include the SOS Assistance Group (800-523-8662 or www.internationalsos.com) and Medex (800-732-5309 or www.medexassist.com).

40. Stop all home deliveries and notify local law officials: If all family members are traveling with you, make sure you stop the newspaper and mail delivery. Make sure trusted neighbors know your basic travel plans and are alerted to anyone who has access to the premises—gardeners, repair people, family or friends, etc. It's also wise to contact the local police or sheriff's department to give them the same travel itinerary and access information. Many local law enforcement agencies offer increased drive-by security checks when you travel extensively. If not, ask or hire a neighbor to make frequent security checks on your residence.

41. Take along extra medicine: If you take any medication regularly, take at least one week's extra supply with you. If your medication is a registered narcotic, make sure you have a letter with you from your doctor. Carry all necessary medication with you in your carry-on luggage—purse, briefcase, backpack, etc. Never place immediately needed medication in your checked luggage. If it's lost or stolen, you could end up with a medical emergency and virtually no chance to get your prescription replaced quickly.

42. Carry an extra pair of glasses and contact lenses with you: Whether traveling domestically or internationally, it's a good insurance policy to carry an extra pair of any prescription glasses or contact lenses with you in your briefcase or purse. In addition, it's wise to carry along a signed prescription from your optometrist or local eye doctor so you can quickly secure replacement glasses or contacts throughout the nation or even the world.

43. Check to see if immunizations are required: Most major nations require only standard immunizations and shots. However, if you're traveling to a nation off the beaten path, special shots and inoculations are likely to be required. You can access the Centers for Disease Control (CDC) by calling 800-232-4636, or go to their very comprehensive website at www.cdc.gov/travel. They have a list of all countries' up-to-date vaccination requirements and special disease warnings. Just make sure you allow time for unusual shots or vaccinations, as most doctors seldom have them on hand. Also, some inoculation shots not only hurt like hell, but some may even have side effects such as fever, nausea, body aches, skin rash, etc.

44. Prepare a traveler's survival kit: Take a few items with you when traveling to remote areas, such as a small first aid kit, sun block, antiseptic spray or cream for cuts and scrapes, anti-itch cream for bug bites and skin rashes, water purification tablets, and over-the-counter remedies such as an anti-diarrhea treatment, aspirin, insect repellent, antibiotic eye drops, and lip balm.

It may sound ridiculous, but airport security screening machines can sometimes be triggered and give a "false positive" reading on passengers using certain suntan lotions, skin creams, and even shampoos and conditioners. If the alarm goes off on you, expect to be taken to a secured back room for a much more thorough screening! If you are planning on airline travels, you may want to avoid all the fancy personal care/bath products the day before your departure.

45. Be selective when choosing an airline for travel: All domestic and international airlines offer security. All airlines that operate in and out of the United States must meet minimum Federal Aviation Administration (FAA) standards. Unfortunately, some foreign carriers that operate out of their home country and service regional markets have severe security gaps and loopholes. Malaysia Airlines Flight MH370 disappeared on its way to Beijing, China, back on March 8, 2014 with 238 people on board. Many say its disappearance may be attributed to lax security in passenger screen-

Airline security and aircraft maintenance for all flights originating or leaving the United States undergo some of the most stringent rules and regulations found anywhere in the world. Airlines that are country-specific and do not fly in to or out of the United States do not necessarily have the same regulations related to security or even aircraft safety repairs and upgrades. Check the safety records of those airlines before you book your travels.
Photo courtesy of U.S. Department of State.

ing. A Russian Metrojet airliner (Flight 9268) crashed into the Sinai desert of Egypt on October 31, 2015 and killed all 224 people on board. The radical Muslim terrorist group ISIS (Islamic State in Iraq and Syria) has claimed that they brought the airliner down with a bomb made from a soda pop can filled with explosives.

46. Check out airlines overall safety record and fleet age: There's no question that U.S. and international airlines are continuing to use older jets. However, most carriers overhaul, rebuild, and upgrade all their jets every three to five years. Approximately 60 percent of the population has a fear or unease of flying; this is otherwise known as aviophobia. For most people it comes down to feeling as though they have no control over the situation, coupled with claustrophobia. And while it's nearly impossible to determine how old your actual aircraft is, you can see the overall safety record and service rating and fleet age of aircraft type of dozens of individual airlines by using the Airline Ratings website at www.airlineratings.com. According to their report, Qantas (Australia) has the youngest fleet of aircraft with an average age of 7.9 years.

47. Consider chartering a flight: Following the rash of terrorist or criminal attacks directed toward major airline carriers or international airports, many of the major Fortune 500 companies decided the best way to protect the organization and its top corporate executives was to bring out the corporate jets or hire special charter flights. Both add a lot more security for travel, though they are extremely expensive.

48. Avoid stopovers: Always plan your travel by taking the most direct route available. If stopovers are required, try to ensure they are few. Every time your plane lands and takes on new passengers and luggage, the risk of an incident rises accordingly.

49. Take as few credit cards as possible: Take only the credit/ATM cards with you that you are going to need and use, cleaning your wallet or purse before you travel domestically or internationally. Wallet and purse theft are some of the top crimes against travelers here and abroad. It's better to have two to five credit cards stolen and reported than perhaps a dozen, in which case you may not even know what cards are missing!

50. Consider credit card/ID theft protection: If your credit cards are lost or stolen, it might be easier if you belong to a centralized credit card/anti-ID theft protection group. Companies such as Identity Guard (www.identityguard.com), LifeLock (www.lifelock.com), or even AARP (www.aarpidprotection.com) have programs that protect their members domestically and internationally.

51. Double-check your departure time: Whether you're flying domestically or internationally, it's wise to call the airline and the airport to make sure your departure flight is on time. This can not only save you time and the inconvenience of arriving at the airport too early, but it can also help you avoid exposing yourself to risk by sitting around for hours. However, with new security regulations, you'd better get a good book (like this one) to read! Plan to be at the airport two or three hours in advance for domestic flights and up to five hours for international flights.

Regardless of domestic or international travel destinations, make sure that you double-check and even triple-check your departure times. Plan to arrive three hours before domestic flights, and four to five hours for any international departures. Flights are often canceled or delayed because of mechanical, weather, and even pilot or flight attendant issues.

52. Park off-site from airports: Parking on-site at airports is often more expensive than parking in more remote or off-site lots. On-site areas are usually crowded and are often target areas for tourist bandits looking to steal baggage or even to rob and assault travelers. Off-site parking areas offer cheaper rates for daily and weekly parking, shuttle buses from your parking spot directly to the terminal, and curbside luggage assistance.

53. Think twice about traveling first class: Although traveling first class is always a lot nicer than squeezing into the back of the coach section, first-class areas on ships and airplanes are traditionally the first areas to be taken over by terrorists. First-class passengers are identified as being wealthy and are usually the last to be released by terrorists in any sort of hijacking situation.

54. Contact the U.S. State Department for Travel Alerts/Warnings: For the official word on criminal and terrorist advisories while traveling abroad, travelers need to enlist the resources of the U.S. government. Basic information and travel advisories can be accessed twenty-four hours a day by going to their very comprehensive website, www.travel.state.gov. On that site, you simply type in the name of the country you are planning on visiting, and it will link you directly to the latest status information available, complete with any Travel Warnings and Alerts.

A Travel Warning is exactly that! A warning about whether you should even consider going to that country at all! A Travel Alert is aimed at notifying travelers about any short-term events that should be considered when planning a visit.

55. Register with Smart Traveler Enrollment Program (STEP): In the old days, it was strongly advised to register with the U.S. embassy or consulate general's office once you arrived in a foreign country. This way, the U.S. government knew that you had arrived, where you were staying, how long you would be in country, and they would have a way of contacting you in the event of an emergency. Today, you can take care of most all of those details in advance of your travels by simply registering with the U.S. State Department's Smart Traveler Enrollment Program (STEP), on their website at: https://step.state.gov/step/. Not only is it suggested that you register yourself and any travel companions, but your family, friends, and business associates can also register and receive any important notifications.

56. TSA Pre√® Expedited Security Screening: If you are a frequent flyer/traveler, you may want to consider enrolling in the Transportation Security Administration's TSA Pre√® program. It is an expedited security screening program for trusted travelers, but you must apply and be accepted. The program has an $85 fee and it is valid for travel for five years. It allows for shorter security line checkpoints and there is no need to remove your shoes, belt, light jacket, laptop or the 3-1-1 liquids. (The 3-1-1 rule for liquids means that you can carry in your carry-on bag a one-quart clear plastic bag, with a maximum of 3.4 ounces or 100 milliliters of liquids, aerosols, gels, creams or pastes through the checkpoint.)

The Transportation Security Administration's TSA Pre√® program is available at more than 150 airports with twelve participating airlines. You can apply in person or start the process at https://www.tsa.gov/precheck.

3

TIPS FOR PROTECTING YOUR LUGGAGE

The days of packing everything you want and simply putting a lock on your luggage are a thing of the past. Today, you not only have to be careful about what items you need for your trip (while still worrying about theft and tampering), but you have to be informed on the proper ways to secure your bags!

57. Locking your luggage: Whether you are traveling domestically or internationally, all luggage is going to be screened. At minimum, expect your luggage to be screened via electronic scanners. If the Transportation Security Administration (TSA) determines that your luggage needs to be physically inspected, they will open the bag, regardless of whether it has a lock on it or not!

If those bags are locked with standard luggage locks, the TSA inspector is permitted to break the lock to inspect the luggage, and then place a notice inside your bag to inform you of the inspection. Some luggage manufacturers make approved locks that TSA screeners can open and not have to break into. As a cheap alternative, you can secure your bags with plastic cables or zip-ties. TSA officials can then simply snip the cables or zip-ties for access to your luggage. Carry extra zip-ties in your carry-on luggage so you can replace them if you notice that they have been snipped and checked, and you can secure them again on your return home. Or you can purchase TSA-approved locks that bear either the Travel Sentry (www.travelsentry.org) or Safe Skies (www.safeskieslocks.com) logo, which is recognized by TSA screeners here in the United States. Of course, you then have to hope that foreign country luggage inspectors won't have the same keys! These locks, which are sold by luggage companies, retail stores, and on the Internet, come in a variety of colors, patterns, and styles that make it easier to identify your bags. Combination locks have a master key lock system that only a TSA official has, allowing inspectors to access your luggage and not break the locks. Professional thieves often have more keys to open your luggage locks than you do. Combo locks are the best choice! Have the combination written down and tucked away with your important travel documents. If the lock is broken by the TSA screener, Safe Skies and Travel Sentry will replace the lock at no charge. Another alternative is either soft or hard-sided luggage that is sold with

When traveling, your checked luggage needs to be secured and locked to prevent everything from theft to the danger of terrorists planting dangerous items. Unfortunately, unless the locks are approved and have an "official" Transportation Security Administration (TSA) security access system, all your regular luggage locks are going to be cut off. TSA approved locks allow access for security checks by baggage inspectors and can be relocked when the inspection is completed. TSA locks are available at most luggage shops, big-box stores, and through the Internet.

a pre-installed TSA-approved lock system.

58. Use baggage seals: Locks are a great idea, but you may also want to add additional security straps. Available through many mail-order travel catalogs, luggage stores, retail outlets, and on the Internet, these straps wrap around and then lock around your luggage. Often sporting bright colors and designs, they can aid you in quickly identifying your luggage and alerting you to the possibility that someone has tampered with your bags. Safe Skies (www. safeskieslocks.com) make these type of luggage straps, available with a combination lock, which you can use to prevent luggage from accidentally opening.

Here are some simple dos and don'ts when it comes to luggage identification tags. Do not use luggage tags that can identify you or your occupation. Showing you are associated with a U.S. defense contractor, a member of the military, have connections with a firearms manufacturer, etc. should be  avoided. Use an airline-provided fold-up tag or your own. Always use your work address on the tag if possible. Home addresses can tell criminals that you are not at home! Also place your identification information inside your checked luggage, as it makes it easier to identify and return to you if lost while you are traveling.

59. Use fold-over luggage ID tags: Open tags allow prying eyes to immediately identify you and where you are from. In addition to the danger of terrorism, airport criminals can instantly tell that you and your family will be out of town. Your residence is likely to be uninhabited, vacant, and vulnerable.

60. Use nondescript luggage tags: Never use your business card as a luggage tag. It tells too much about you. Use airport-available fold-over luggage tags with your name, office address and office telephone number only.

61. Avoid those "special" airline and hotel custom luggage tags: Luggage tags from major airline or hotel chains may be a sign of status for today's business traveler, but they are also a tip-off to terrorists or criminals that you are a frequent traveler, wealthy, or that you work for a wealthy company or corporation. High-visibility and high-profile luggage tags from airlines and hotel chains are best accepted graciously and then left back at the home or office.

62. Remove travel and business stickers from all your bags: Keep your luggage (check-in and carry-on) clean of all stickers that indicate where you have traveled or worked. Stickers such as "Go Navy," "Boeing Aircraft Company," and even "I Love New York" need to be removed. They can identify you as military, wealthy, etc.

Eliminate and clean your luggage or suitcases of all identifying stickers and labels. One look at this example of what not to do tells a would-be terrorist or criminal WAY too much about your personal life and your American affiliations.

63. Learn to pack carry-on luggage for security checks: Due to increased security checks, there will be no secrets in your carry-on luggage. Expect that any and all carry-on electronic devices—computers, cell phones, radios, printers, and even shavers or beard trimmers—are going to be spotted and hand-searched after they go through the standard x-ray security check. Because of these additional checks, you can expect everything from dirty underwear and smelly socks to sexy lingerie and adult DVDs/magazines will be subject to search, inspection, and review.

You are allowed to bring a *single* quart-sized bag of liquids, aerosols, gels, creams, and pastes in your carry-on bag and through the security checkpoint. These are limited to travel-sized containers that are 3.4 ounces (100 milliliters) or less per item. Placing these items in the small bag and separating from your other carry-on bag/bags facilitates the screening process. Pack items that are in containers larger than 3.4 ounces or 100 milliliters in your checked baggage. Best advice is to take little or nothing through security! Any liquid, aerosol, gel, cream, or paste that catches notice during screening will require additional screening or be confiscated.

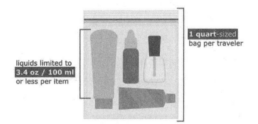

Carrying any liquids aboard an airliner today in your carry-on luggage can be a real pain! Most seasoned travelers will likely purchase shampoos, toothpastes, hand creams, and eye drops at their final destination. TSA limits travelers to a 1 quart-sized bag per traveler and liquids inside that zipped/ sealed bag are limited to 3.4 ounces/100 milliliters or less per each item. Illustration courtesy of TSA.

64. Learn to pack checked luggage for security checks: As new security checks on everything from domestic to international baggage are increased, expect that your suitcases may be screened and looked at closely as part of regular travel. Pack so any and all electrical devices can be accessed quickly on the top of your luggage—electric razors, beard trimmers, CD/DVD players, computer accessories, external modems, electronic notebooks, tablets, or hair dryers, curling irons, styling brushes and all other personal devices.

65. "Electric pencil" your valuables: If you're taking a camera, video camera, computer, cell phone or any other such valuables with you on your travels, use an electric pencil to engrave your telephone number on all your gear. If you're traveling internationally, you might also be wise to inscribe "USA" under any identification numbers. Never inscribe your Social Security number on anything! If these items are stolen, electric penciling makes it harder for the thief to pawn them, and makes it easier, if the item is ever recovered by the police, to identify it as yours.

66. "Sanitize" your identification: Do not carry your business cards, military identification, or anything nonessential with you. Put all this material in your checked bags if you must carry it. When traveling, carry only your driver's license, passport, and the few credit cards you plan to use on your trip.

67. Dress up your wallet and purse: Add pictures of family, grandma, and children—the more the better—even if you are single. This may seem somewhat outlandish, but if a terrorist or criminal grabs your wallet or purse and sees photos showing that you have a large family it may create a sympathy factor. If you become a hostage, it might even safe your life!

68. Divide up the valuables: If you are traveling with family members, split up the cash and credit cards. This way if someone is robbed or luggage is lost, then you and your family are not totally wiped out for the trip.

69. Check your reading material: Don't carry any controversial reading material with you. This includes gun magazines, religious books, material critical of world leaders, swimsuit magazines, or anything else that a terrorist group might find repulsive or antagonistic.

When traveling, especially internationally, you have to be aware of how you present yourself, and that today even includes carrying any sort of controversial reading material. Firearm or fashion magazines, religious books, and political writings are best left at home. Hit the local bookstore at the airport and buy a novel or a newspaper.

70. Pack defensive tools: Nobody is suggesting that all travelers become an armed citizen—that's the job of professional sky marshals and other authorities. However, it's good insurance to take your cell phone, cell phone charger with cord, your PDA, your laptop computer, or even a hard-cover book along with you. Most all sharp objects—money clip knives, nail files, metal scissors, etc.—are now illegal to take onboard domestic or international flights. But even a stout ink pen can make an effective weapon in fending off an attack in an emergency. You can review all the prohibited items—*and there are a lot of them*—in chapter 15 of this book or on the TSA website at www.tsa.gov/travel/security-screening/prohibited-items.

71. Keep your travel papers separate: Do not carry your ground itinerary and travel tickets together. If lost or stolen, this can tell criminals too much about your travel plans.

4

TIPS FOR SAFETY AT AIRPORTS

Airport terminals, airline counters, and even baggage claim areas are extremely vulnerable to bombings, shootings, theft, etc. Plan to get through those "non-secured" areas as quickly as possible.

 Remember the good ol' days when airline travel was fun? Unfortunately, those days are pretty much over, with everything from overbooked airlines to demanding security concerns. Smart travelers today have to do a lot more advance planning in order to have any sort of "non-drama" journeys!

72. Check in early: Not only should you get to the airport early enough to avoid all the long check-in lines and increased security checks, but it's wise to clear the front check-in areas as quickly as possible. As was seen in the ISIS attack at the Brussels airport in March 2016, which killed fourteen people and injured ninety-two, the fronts of airports are often nothing short of death traps! If you are standing in line for a long period of time at the check-in counter, you increase the risk of danger. Savvy travelers will arrive three hours before domestic flights, while international travelers will make sure they arrive at least four to five hours before their departure times. *And then get through security and deep inside the terminal!*

The departure area of any airport is usually located close to where passengers and vehicles are often milling about. They usually have lots of glass and little security. Get to the airport early enough to avoid crowds and long lines, get through the departure check-in area as quickly as possible, and move through security and deeper into the airport as soon as possible. Numerous attacks can make the departure and arrival areas a terrorist death trap! Suicide bombers in Belgium and Turkey are two of the latest attacks that took place in the departure and arrival and baggage claim areas.

73. Use curbside baggage assistance if available: It used to be that all you had to do was show a ticket, an ID, and a tip . . . and your bags were tagged and whisked aboard for you. As you likely know well, this is no longer the case. Today, about the best you can hope for is that the luggage handlers will help you load your bags onto their carts and then escort you to your airline check-in counter. Even that assistance can help you save your aching back!

74. Remember, even though you have pre-assigned seating, you must still check in: It doesn't matter how far in advance you booked your ticket and received your seat assignment, it won't be reserved for the flight until you actually check in either at the terminal entrance, and sometimes again at the gate.

75. Try to select the safest seats: Government and airline studies cannot show what exact areas onboard an aircraft offer the safest seating in the event of an emergency landing or crash. Sometimes the best seats are up front, and other times they are in the rear. However, in the event of a terrorist hijacking, the best seats for protection are located at the windows or center seats. Passengers least exposed to killings and beatings during a hijacking were in those seats, located in the mid and aft sections. Terrorists are most often up front near the cockpit area, first class, and front doors.

While many travelers believe that sitting in the aft or back of the airplane is safest while traveling, statistics simply show that is not always true. Window seats provide the best view, but in the event of an emergency it may be more difficult to wait or climb over other passengers when heading to an emergency exit. Sitting on the aisle may give you the most leg/arm room, but it also puts you closest to a hijacker/crazy in the event of crisis.

76. Buy airport travel insurance: If you didn't increase your insurance policies for personal and property protection before you left home, through your personal insurance agent or purchasing it on the Internet, you may still have one last chance to secure the coverage you need. It's going to be appreciably more expensive, but you can cover yourself and all your luggage by putting the special travel insurance on your credit card. Many major airports have insurance-selling kiosks and machines located inside the terminals.

77. Beware of carry-on baggage check thieves: Keep your carry-on luggage with you until you are ready to go through the metal detector. Organized thieves—*and, yes, they do buy tickets to be able to go through security*—are good at slowing down the walk-through metal detector lines while your bags go through the x-ray scanners. When you get to the other side, your bag with all your personal papers, computer, etc. are gone! Don't put them on the x-ray machine until you are about to enter, and keep your eyes on your bags or bins! Computer cases and camera bags are easy prey for thieves.

78. Do not sit near large plate glass windows in the terminal: Exploding glass can be as deadly as a bomb blast itself. Always sit in the middle of the terminal area with your back up against a solid wall or pillar and your back to the windows.

79. Stay away from the gate: Do not sit near the gate where your plane is going to depart from until you hear the boarding announcement. Airline gates are notorious terrorist and thief targets.

80. Consider joining airline clubs: These clubs are by membership only and they require an additional identification check to enter. They are usually far enough from the boarding gate to add to your security. The annual cost to join is between $400 and $600 per year—and if you are a frequent traveler or have enough airline miles built up in your account you can get substantial discounts or even use your banked mileage for memberships.

81. Get baggage assistance at your destination: Upon arrival at your destination, allow the baggage handlers to carry your luggage to your ground transportation. It can often speed you through the luggage areas and adds a built-in escort to your car, shuttle, or taxi.

82. Pre-arrange for ground transportation: If possible, try to arrange for your ground transportation in advance so that it's waiting for you upon arrival. Limo services are good in terms of being prompt, but they can also identify you as a wealthy business traveler. Many travelers are now using the services of Uber drivers (www.uber.com) where you can use your smartphone to arrange for a car and driver to pick you up at the airport, hotel or other location at an assigned time and pre-pay for it with your credit card. You not only have a picture of the driver sent to you when you make your reservations, you can also order the car to be anything from a non-descript economy sedan up to a stretch limo! Uber operates in over four hundred cities worldwide.

83. Avoid hailing a taxi: Waiting in a long taxi line, or trying to hail one yourself, can be dangerous. The possibility of a drive-by attack or a criminal assault is always there. If possible, hire a baggage handler to get a cab for you.

84. Examine your luggage: When your bags arrive at the baggage claim area, examine them carefully. Are all the locks still in place? Has a bag been opened or does it appear to have been tampered with? If so, do not touch it—call security immediately for help.

85. Handle luggage problems as soon as possible: Most domestic and international airlines require all luggage complaints be made either before you leave the airport, or within four hours of your flight's arrival. Domestic airline liability for damage to luggage or theft to its contents is limited to approximately $3,400—provided you can back up your claims with receipts. On international flights it's a varying rate per passenger for checked baggage based on the

Warsaw Convention or the Montreal Convention. Check with your international airline carrier.

86. Stay away from unattended luggage: Avoid piles of luggage, unattended bags, boxes, or parcels. Any one of them could contain an explosive. If you see abandoned bags or boxes, get away immediately and call security. Remember, "if you see something, say something!"

Unattended luggage could easily be a planted explosive, even one placed in the baggage claim area, looking like it might have been forgotten by a traveler. If you see luggage without someone close by, report it immediately to airport security!

87. Expect all international airlines will match luggage to each passenger: It may be a time-consuming process, but making sure all bags loaded onto the airplane are linked to passengers greatly reduces the chance that a dangerous package will be stowed aboard.

88. Look around for suspicious individuals: Be observant of people who are around you—anyone could be a pickpocket, luggage thief, or even a terrorist. If you are in doubt about suspicious individuals or actions, call security.

89. Drop to the ground if there are any threat warnings: If you hear anything that sounds like gunfire or an explosion, immediately fall flat on the ground and cover your head. Do not run or panic. Remember: *it is impossible to outrun flying bullets or exploding shrapnel.*

Bomb Threat Stand-Off Evacuation Distances

Mandatory

Device	Distance
Pipe Bomb	70 ft/21 m
Suicide Vest	110 ft/34 m
Briefcase/Suitcase	150 ft/46 m
Sedan	320 ft/98 m
SUV/Van	400 ft/122 m
Small Delivery Truck	640 ft/195 m
Container Truck	860 ft/263 m
Semi-Trailer	1,570 ft/479 m

Explosive attacks against innocent people are a favorite weapon of terrorists, and can have long-range and deadly effects to great distances. If you hear an explosion or gunfire, your first line of defense is to drop to the ground and immediately seek cover. Chart courtesy of NCTC.

5

SAFETY ABOARD THE AIRPLANE, CRUISE SHIP, TOUR BUS

Even after all the hassles of clearing security and getting on board your airplane, cruise ship, or tour bus, it pays to be observant and vigilant about your surroundings and others that are also traveling.

90. Time changes and jet lag: Traveling even relatively short distances via plane, boat, or bus with time changes can cause your body to suffer from jet lag—tiredness, sleepiness, body aches, constipation, etc. Try to adjust your schedule a few days before your travels to begin compensating for this. Drink more liquids, cut back on smoking and alcohol, get more sleep earlier or later, and so on.

When you arrive at your destination, give your body a chance to acclimate to the time changes. Don't try to "hit the ground running" and plan too many activities, especially the first day.

91. Seat selection = crash protection: Fire and smoke are the biggest problems in a survivable crash, even if you are on an airplane, rail car, or travel bus. Selecting a window or aisle seat near a door or emergency exit can make getting out of the aircraft, rail car, or bus quickly much easier.

All commercial aircraft around the world have multiple emergency exits. Know where the two closest ones are to your seat. Take the time to look at the Emergency Card that is located in the seat pocket in front of you, so that you know where the exits are, how to operate the doors, emergency slides, seat cushion/flotation device, etc.

92. If a crash seems imminent: Tighten your seat belt around your hips as tight as possible and brace your feet against the leg frame of the seat in front of you. Bend over so that your head is down on your knees, and use your arms to cradle around your head for additional protection. Use pillows, blankets, or your coat to add more cushion.

93. Fire and smoke protection: In the event of a fire, use a scarf, blanket, napkin, or cloth to cover your nose and mouth. Relatively inexpensive portable smoke hoods with ventilators, stowed easily in your carry-on luggage for airline travel, or in your luggage when taking a cruise ship, can be an extra insurance policy against heat and smoke danger caused by fire. On the airplane, rail car, or bus, count the number of rows to the nearest emergency exit before departure. In a cabin filled with smoke, that information could save your life. On a cruise liner, know where your cabin is located in regards to emergency exits, fire extinguishers, water hoses, etc.

94. Evaluate passengers around you: It is important to be observant of who is sitting next to you and around you. Discreetly notify the flight crew, the tour bus driver, your guide, rail car conductor, or the ship's crew if you see anything suspicious. You may nowadays be called upon to help and assist. Evaluate other passengers ahead of time to see who might be able to join you in helping during an emergency.

95. Check your seat: Give your seat a security check—don't rely on the aircraft ground crews, bus driver, etc. Check the seat pocket in front of you; lean forward and look under your seat for packages, wires, or suspicious bulges. Check the overhead luggage bin for forgotten or planted packages. After 9/11, a couple of box-cutter knives were not discovered aboard one aircraft until nearly two weeks after the other attacks. And because there is less security on trains and buses, they are often used to "stash" contraband that you do not want to be associated with!

Safety on board your airplane should begin the moment you get to your assigned seat area. Check your surroundings for any suspicious "left-on-board" packages or parcels. Look in the overhead luggage bins, in the seat pocket, and even under your seat. If you see something that  is not what you brought with you on the plane, notify a flight attendant immediately.

96. Use "stash" areas: Look around for areas within arm's reach to conceal any materials or documents you must carry, but do not want found or associated with you. Usually the seat cushion that you are sitting on is the best place to hide papers quickly.

97. "Bad vibrations": Don't overreact, but don't ignore that "sixth sense" either. If you have a bad feeling about passengers around you, about the plane, or about the rail car or bus, consider getting off. Even if you have a special-fare ticket, in most cases major airline carriers, train lines, and tour companies will try to accommodate your concerns about safety or apprehensiveness.

98. Heated discussions: Avoid heated or emotional discussions with fellow passengers. Arguing about politics, religion, races, or other related topics will win you few points when traveling. If you disagree, it is best to sit and remain silent. Put on your stereo headphones and watch the movie or listen to music.

6

SAFETY AT YOUR DESTINATION AND WHILE TRAVELING

Once you've arrived at your destination, or if you are planning additional travels, remember that you and only you are going to be able to continue to protect yourself from terrorism or criminal activity. Be alert!

Virtually all nations have increased security against terrorism in their countries, but it is doubtful that it can stop all attacks and incidents. Travelers today have to take much more responsibility for themselves and be alert to their surroundings and what is going on around them. Remember, there is no 100 percent safety guarantee! Modern terrorists and criminals are always looking for security flaws.
Photo courtesy of NCTC.

99. Hotel driveways: If driving to your hotel, stay with your car and luggage until a bellman or doorman arrives to assist you. Many travelers simply drive up, pop the trunk button, and head inside to check in. Many are equally surprised to return and find everything from their luggage to their car gone upon their return.

100. Hotel check-in: In many nations, and even at many domestic hotels, it is customary for the bellman to take your bags from your car and deliver them to your room later. Unless all bags are locked, it's unwise to let your luggage leave your sight. Not only do you run the risk of theft, but a bomb could be planted in your bags and timed to explode once they arrive in your room.

101. Room number security: Most hotels have done away with the traditional room key and have adopted systems for electronic keys. If your key—be it brass or electronic—has your room number on it, make sure you keep it covered and away from prying eyes. And if the check-in people announce your room number while handing you your key, you might want to consider immediately asking for another room. Prying ears are just as much a concern as the prying eyes of those who may wish to do you harm.

102. Credit card imprints versus cash checkouts: If the check-in clerk asks for your credit card for an imprint to cover incidental expenses—room service, movie charges, telephone calls, gift shop, etc.—and you pay cash upon checkout, make sure your credit card imprint is destroyed in front of you at that time. Many hotels will offer you expedited check-out service if you do not physically need a copy of your hotel charges. Time permitting, however, it is a good idea to get a copy of your bill when checking out. This way, you know everything is closed out and have a copy of all charges. Hotel employees, especially in foreign countries, have been known to pocket your cash payments and still put the hotel charges back on your credit card.

103. Office address at hotel check-ins: When checking in at any hotel or motel, give your office address (but not company name), or post office box instead of your home address information. Be careful about giving out any home address information to "friendly locals" you might meet. They could be part of a crime gang that targets travelers' residences while away from home. If you want to stay in touch, give them your office address and phone numbers. Or better yet . . . email!

104. Unscheduled meetings: Avoid meeting strangers, even for a "friendly" drink or meal, at any secluded or unknown location. Arrange for necessary meetings to take place at a location you are familiar with.

105. Request a room on the concierge level: Many hotels have floors set aside for frequent business travelers. These business travelers' levels and concierge floors usually require special elevator access. It adds an extra level of security in addition to often complimentary breakfasts and places to hold meetings in a secure lounge area.

Many of the larger hotel chains (domestic and abroad) have a concierge floor or lounge for their frequent guests. Check out requirements for upgrading to that level if available. It is usually a floor that requires a special key to access and adds to overall security during your stay. Most also have  a private lounge that is more secure for relaxing or having a meeting with business clients than the lobby areas and bars. They also are likely to have great snacks and hors d'oeuvres during daily happy hour.

106. Room requests: Request a room toward the back of the hotel and away from the front entrance and lobby area. Attacks against hotels are almost always directed at the front of these buildings. Higher levels are also better protected against blast damage by the virtue of being further away from low-level lobby or car bombs. The sweet spot is the fourth or fifth floor—above that level, there is a concern about fire danger, especially in many foreign hotels where smoke detectors, fire sprinklers, and emergency lighting and exits are not mandated.

Car bombs and planted explosives have continued to be a favorite weapon of today's terrorists. Modern explosives are a lot more powerful than TNT and have enabled bombers to make explosive devices that are often 10–100 times more powerful and destructive.
Photo courtesy of NCTC.

107. In-room safe-deposit boxes: Many hotels now have in-room safes, that you can rent to store your valuables such as jewelry, papers, tickets, money, extra glasses, prescription medicines, etc. Most are programmable with your own personally selected combination. Don't leave anything valuable in your hotel room. However, if you are not planning on using the safe in your room, let them know when you check in, and the daily fee might be subtracted from your bill when you check out.

If your hotel only provides safe deposit boxes or the hotel's main safe, ask about the hotel's insurance coverage policy. If you use the hotel's main safe, make sure you get a written, detailed, and signed receipt for the all the items you are storing.

108. Keep your key: Some hotels—especially small ones and bed-

and-breakfasts in foreign nations—ask you to turn in your room key when you are going outside the hotel. *Do not!* Placed in an open-front key box or hung on a hook it alerts everyone that your room is unoccupied. Keep your key with you at all times.

109. Check your room: Whenever you return to your hotel room, stand in the doorway and look inside before entering. Is everything the way it was left? If not, leave immediately and notify hotel staff and security.

Whenever you come back to your hotel room, check it out when entering and make sure that everything is pretty much the way you left it in terms of personal items, etc. If your personal items, luggage, or papers are "tossed," leave the room immediately and notify security. Rooms located toward the back of the hotel/motel are usually safer from crime or terrorists than those located near the front entrance.

110. Leave your room neat: Yes, you may be on vacation, but keep the room tidy. Pick up clothes and arrange business papers in neat piles. Sweep all the hotel advertising into a drawer. That way you will be able to tell if closets, papers, or personal items have been searched.

111. Ensure privacy: Unless your room needs servicing, whenever you leave your hotel room, leave the radio or television on at an audible level. Also leave a light on in your room when going out, and always hang out the Do Not Disturb sign. This makes the room seem occupied.

112. Room security devices: Obviously your hotel room should be locked and dead-bolted at all times when you are in the room.

While at your hotel or motel, always put out the Do Not Distrub sign on your door until you are ready to have your room cleaned. Hanging that little plastic sign is a warning to any robber, burglar, or other intruder that the room is likely to be occupied. Most bad guys want to avoid any face-to-face confrontation and will seek out an easier target.

However, you may want to increase that security level by using a lightweight but sturdy "door-stop" device or a portable alarm that hangs from the doorknob and sounds if the door is opened. These and other devices are often available through a host of mail-order catalogs on the Internet and even through many airline in-flight magazines.

113. Never open your hotel door unless it's expected: The Automobile Association of America (AAA) has dropped all hotels and motels from its recommended listings for establishments that do not provide dead-bolts and peepholes on all hotel room doors. Use these devices and never answer the door without verifying who's there. Accept no unexpected flowers, fruit baskets, room service, or maid service unless the hotel guest services desk can confirm it.

Never loiter in or around the hotel entrance. Move your luggage inside as quickly as possible. Hotel entrances usually have minimal security and everything from bag-snatching criminals to drive-by shootings can and do happen. Let the bellman take care of the bags from your car, taxi, or shuttle. Get to the check-in counter and away from the front doors.

114. Do not arrange meetings in the lobby: Avoid the hotel lobby and lobby bars, even for short visits. This is a very high-target area for car bombs, unattended bag bombs, shootings, and pickpockets. If you are to meet someone, get together by the elevators, in front of the health club, swimming pool, or other out-of-the way area.

115. Low-profile bars and restaurants: Avoid the popular and trendy bars, restaurants, discos, etc. if you're in an area where terror tension is high. Top targets in the Paris attack (November 2015) were popular restaurants/bistros and outside cafés/bars. Try some of the offbeat local pubs and eateries instead. They are generally safer and will enhance your enjoyment of the local "flavor" as well.

Local cafés, bistros, and restaurants that offer outside dining that are on small streets and not facing busy tourist boulevards and attractions are less likely to be targets of attack or criminal activity. After visiting major tourist attractions, the quiet of getting away from all the other tourists and visitors might be a welcome respite!

116. Carry a local newspaper: Even if it is in a language you don't know, it is an effective deception in lowering your profile as a tourist in another country and looking more like a local.

117. Keep abreast of local and international news: Turn on the television or radio and pick up both a local and international newspaper. If you're traveling internationally, it's important to know what's happening throughout the world.

118. Vary your schedule: This includes routes, travel destinations, and times. Do not continue to predictably leave at 8:00 a.m. and return at 5:00 p.m. day after day.

119. Hotel entrances/exits: Know where all the hotel entrances and exits are in your area. Don't continually enter and exit through the main hotel entrance. Sometimes use the side exits. If someone is watching you for your arrival and departure, it makes it more difficult to know your schedule.

120. Emergency exits: Know where all the emergency exits are in your hotel and even in the office building or convention center you are visiting. Make a mental note as to where the fire extinguishers or hoses are located. At your hotel, count the number of doors from your room to the nearest emergency exit. In the event of fire, you may have to crawl through heavy smoke. Also learn how to get out of restaurants, stores, theaters, and sporting events quickly.

121. U.S. cell phones in foreign countries: Cell phones used routinely here in the United States are generally not compatible with foreign nation's cell phone frequencies or systems. Check with your cell phone provider to see if yours can be adapted for foreign travel. If you do not have a "locked" phone, you can often purchase a postage stamp-sized SIM (subscriber identity module) for overseas use. Beware that the rates you pay per minute can be all over the chart. Make sure that you also know about any roaming fees and extra charges. Some frequent travelers simply opt to purchase a cheap phone with an international SIM card.

A reliable cell phone is a must for the modern traveler. Check with your cell-phone carrier to ensure that it will operate at your destination, especially when traveling abroad. If not, see about purchasing or renting one when you arrive. Many phones today also include everything from GPS navigation software to one-touch panic buttons. Both are great features to have for your travel adventures.

122. Hotel telephones and faxes: Telephone charges from hotels are routinely marked up by 100 percent or more on domestic calls. International calls can reflect 200 percent to 300 percent boosts in costs. Avoid these surcharges by placing calls on your cell phone or use an international telephone credit card. Be aware that what you discuss over a hotel telephone can in some cases be monitored. Some governments have wired tourists' rooms for sound. Avoid hotel-delivered faxes that contain sensitive information. It's best to use your laptop computer and the hotel's secure Wi-Fi.

123. Pre-paid telephone calling cards: One of the easiest and still most inexpensive ways to make a long-distance domestic or international telephone call is by using one of the many pre-paid or debit calling cards that are now available through the major phone companies or on the Internet. Cash up front, the card is guaranteed for local, short, and a limited amount of long-distance calling. Even if phone thieves get the number, its use is extremely limited.

124. Unexpected packages: Never accept or offer to carry packages that you are not expecting or do not belong to you. Even if you are expecting a package or parcel, examine it carefully for signs of tampering before you open it.

125. Register your foreign visit with the U.S. embassy or consulate upon arrival at your destination: Hopefully, you have pre-registered your travels with the U.S. State Department's STEP program (Smart Traveler Enrollment Program) at https://step.state.gov/step/. If not, soon after your arrival into any international city/destination, it's well worth the time and trouble to contact the U.S. embassy or consulate and let them know of your travel plans and schedule. Sometimes you can register your visit by telephone from your hotel room, or from your laptop. If trouble breaks out in your area, the U.S. embassy or consulate can contact you with this warning information. Carry the address and telephone number of the embassy or consulate office with you and with all family members at all times.

126. Know how embassies and consulates can be of help: U.S. consulates and embassies can offer limited help and assistance to traveling U.S. citizens. They can alert you in times of political trouble and unrest, assist with replacement passports, help with money transfer, reaching friends and family members, canceling credit cards, and protecting your legal rights. They can't get you out of

Thousands of American travelers are arrested each year while traveling abroad. Remember that other country's laws regarding arrest, detention, and incarceration are likely to be a lot different than here in the good-ol' USA. While the U.S. embassy or consulate in other countries can help you find legal assistance, they will not help you post bail money or get you out of jail!

jail, don't loan money, don't offer replacement airline tickets, or pay for medical emergencies.

127. Take taxis: When traveling around town, take taxis to avoid walking long distances. Take only known and marked taxis, and avoid unmarked cars with unregistered drivers. Too often they can be swindlers or dangerous criminals. If you need daily transport with a driver, allow the hotel guest services to arrange for this service, or see if Uber is available.

128. Use caution with car rental companies: Many rental agencies still have identifying tags and stickers (back of driver's mirror, rear window, bumpers, etc.) and even custom license plate holders that tell every criminal or crazy that you are a traveler in a rental car. If your rental company hasn't removed these "flags," it's time to find a new place to take your business.

129. Rental cars with car phones and locators: Often for only a small extra charge, you can also rent a cellular phone with your rental car. Most are set up with one-button emergency assistance numbers. Some car companies are even installing panic buttons that automatically send out an emergency call that can pinpoint a vehicle's exact location. Also helpful are cell phone apps or rental cars equipped with global positioning system (GPS) receivers that help you navigate via electronic maps wherever you need to go. Trying to navigate with paper maps in an unfamiliar city—domestic or foreign—is archaic and a waste of your time!

130. Plan your routes in advance: Use maps and guidebooks to plan your travels before you leave the hotel. It's good to reconfirm the route with the hotel's guest service manager. They can update you on road closures, construction delays, or routes that will keep

Make sure that you either take your portable, vehicle GPS navigation system with
you, or ensure that one is installed in your
rental vehicle. It is a great safety device for
navigating throughout unfamiliar countries,
U.S. states, and cities around the world. It
saves you looking like a "lost tourist" fumbling with maps or having to continuously
stop and ask for directions. It can also alert
you to construction zones and closed high-
ways. Paper maps can't do that for you!

you out of troubled areas. It then is much easier to plug that information into your GPS system and make sure you are headed in the
right direction.

When traveling domestically or abroad, it is best to do a little advance homework and know where you plan to go in advance. Travelers often make the
mistake of standing out and looking like lost tourists with easy-to-spot guidebooks, maps, etc. Photo courtesy of U.S. Department of State.

131. Pick up rental cars at the hotel and not the airport: Upon
arrival at your domestic or international travel destination, it's far
safer to pick up your rental car at the local hotel than the airport.
Every terrorist or criminal knows where the operating car rental
companies are located. If you arrive late in the evening or at night,
head to the hotel and have the car delivered to you the next day.
It's going to save you from walking out into dark and abandoned

parking lots. In a strange city late at night, it's easy to get lost with a rental car, even if you don't have far to travel.

Securing a rental car at your airport arrival can be a good idea if you are arriving while there is still plenty of daylight, and the car lot is close by. If it is late at night or you have to travel via shuttle bus in the dark, it might be best to see if the rental company will deliver your vehicle to the hotel you are staying at the following morning.

132. Watch your keys: When parking in a garage or parking lot, you may be asked to leave the ignition key in the car or with the attendant. Make sure that if you have luggage or valuables, put them into the trunk yourself—and you take the trunk key with you.

133. Car breakdowns and calls for help: Most rental cars are very mechanically reliable and chances of a breakdown are slim. However, if you do experience a mechanical problem, it's best to stay with the vehicle with the doors locked, windows up, and emergency flashers on. If you've got a cell phone, call for immediate help and don't get out of the vehicle until the identified tow truck or law enforcement officials arrive. Many rentals also now have emergency notification systems on board. Know how to use them!

134. Helping other stranded motorists: In the United States and internationally, it's best not to stop to render assistance for stranded or broken down motorists. Even if someone stands in the road and tries to flag you down, your best assistance is to use your cell phone and call 911. If you don't have a car phone, head to the nearest highly lit and public area to call for assistance on behalf of the motorist who needs help.

135. Avoid big limousines: Traveling back and forth to big hotels, restaurants, and business meetings in attention-drawing stretch limos makes you a high-profile target for criminals or terrorists.

136. Auto accidents: If you're involved in a minor traffic accident or fender bender in an isolated area, do not stop. Turn on your emergency flashers and continue to drive to a well-lit, populated area before you get out of your car to assess the damage and meet with the other driver. Minor accidents are often a cover for robbery or carjacking criminals.

137. Carjackers: If you're faced with a carjacking, it's always best to give the criminals what they want—money, credit cards, and the car you were driving. Locking the doors and windows will do little to stop a criminal's bullets. If the car is equipped with a panic button to summon help, hit it and then get out of the vehicle. If not, let them have any and all physical possessions. You can replace them, but you can't replace your life.

7

LOW-PROFILE TOURISM

Are you a smart, savvy, low-profile traveler? You should be! Blend in with the locals and your surroundings. Don't be an overt or obnoxious tourist!

138. Cameras: Large and bulky cameras should be left at home. Rather than being an obvious tourist, consider purchasing pictures of major sites from a gift store or street vendor. Cell phones now have superior optics and high-resolution options that are as good or even better than those of any pocket camera.

139. See the sights: Most of the major tourist sites are fine to visit. They usually have adequate security if you travel during normal hours. However, as always, be alert to your surroundings and make note of others who might be terrorists or part of a criminal gang. Avoid arriving too early and staying too late.

140. Leave maps/guidebooks in your room: Nothing is more obvious than fumbling with a tourist map on an unfamiliar street.

Plan your route ahead of time—know where you're going and how to get back. Avoid having that "lost" look.

141. Hire private guides: For most tourist areas, private or semi-private tour guides are available and can be arranged through the hotel's guest services. The cost is about one-third more than the group rate in most instances, but the level of security is well worth it. Also, you're likely to enjoy the tour more with the extra personal attention and not feel like you're just another sardine in the can!

Having the opportunity to travel and learn all about the world's history and sites is something virtually everyone treasures. Many travelers are finding that it is safer and more fun to work through their hotel and sign on for small tours to the local sites and attractions, or even hire a private guide. Photo courtesy U.S. Embassy, Turkey.

142. Caution on large organized tours: Large groups of people with the same nationality are often targets of terror and criminal groups. If you decide to join a large tour group, care and caution needs to be exercised throughout, especially getting on and off the large and conspicuous tour buses in front of hotels and at major tourist attractions.

Large tourist buses are easy to spot and are often the target for terrorist shootings and bombings. One way to lower your profile and the threat is to either hire a private car, or sign up with tour companies that use smaller vehicles that are not marked up with logos and destinations. Small buses and vans blend in better with local traffic, and so will you.

143. Offbeat tours: In any country, there are often a variety of "offbeat" tourist attractions and sights. If the major sights are experiencing problems, visit the out-of-the-way places instead. They are often just as interesting sites and landmarks as the major mainstream attractions.

144. Foreign currency exchanges: Exchange your money for local currency only in your hotel, major bank, or designated kiosk. Do not exchange money with local street vendors— it is *illegal* in many countries! Black-market vendors may offer better rates of exchange, but in some nations those vendors are actually undercover law enforcement officers looking to arrest the unwise tourist. The best legitimate exchange rates are going to be found through the major banks.

When you need to secure money, or switch funds to local currency, always use a bank or legitimate financial exchange or kiosk. Street vendors offering better exchange rates can be everything from local criminals setting you up for a robbery, or local law enforcement. Many countries prohibit changing currency outside of banks, and many travelers have been arrested for illegal street transactions!

145. What's your credit limit? Unless you're planning on paying for everything with cash, having a credit card or two with a sizable limit can help with unexpected expenses or emergencies. Do, however, know the credit limits on all credit cards in your possession. Some U.S. citizens have been arrested and detained for going over their credit limits. If you are going to use an ATM/debit card on foreign travels, make sure your hotel and merchants will accept it. Some countries do not allow the use of ATM/debit cards from U.S. banks.

146. U.S. dollars: Don't carry large amounts of U.S. money with you in a foreign country. If you have American dollars, leave them in your in-room hotel safe or the hotel safe deposit box until you can exchange them for local currency. Pulling out a big wad of U.S. greenbacks in any nation and you've automatically identified yourself as a rich American.

147. Smoking: If you've yet to kick the habit, it's wise to see about switching to a local brand of cigars and cigarettes. Domestic U.S. brands in foreign lands can easily identify you as a visitor.

148. Bad neighborhoods: Do not travel into areas where crime is high and police protection is low. Find out from the hotels and restaurants which streets and areas should be avoided. When traveling around a city, make mental notes of safe havens, such as police and fire stations, hospitals, embassies, and the like. Avoid local demonstrations, travel offices, government offices, and other high-visibility target areas.

149. Where did everyone go?: Watch for the conspicuous absence of locals from streets, lobbies, the airport, train station, bus terminal, and so on. It could be an advance warning of a terrorist attack, kidnapping, or bombing.

Sometimes, there are warning signs of a pending bombing or terror attack. If suddenly there are few or no people on the street in an area where it is normally crowded, it could be an indication of a incident that may soon occur. Remember that if you hear an explosion or gunfire, hit the ground and seek cover. Nobody can outrun a bullet or flying shrapnel!
Photo courtesy of NCTC.

150. Watch out for criminal "distractions": If you see a street fight, watch a minor car accident, or have someone accidentally spill mustard on your new suit . . . all of these could be part of a "distraction" process by organized criminals. While your attention is elsewhere, they're extracting your wallet, passport, credit cards, and money.

151. Wallet protection: Wrap a thick rubber band or two around your wallet before you put it in your *front pocket*. It can add a little friction and make it more difficult for a thief to easily slide the wallet out of your pocket. Never carry your wallet, passports, or money in your back pocket unless it has a zipper or button closure. Never carry your wallet or any valuable papers in your jacket or coat. It's simply too easy for an experienced pickpocket to remove these items from you and you'll never know it until they are long gone. Carry important papers, wallet, and money in your front pockets, preferably under a coat or sweater.

152. Money belts: Concealable money belts are better than backpacks, fanny packs, belly pouches, etc. Even safety pinning cash and important papers inside your coat, sweater, or dress is better than carrying everything in your pocket or in a bag. Everything exposed is vulnerable to being grabbed by street thugs. If they grab it, let it go!

153. Destroy all credit card carbons: Some remote areas actually still use the old credit card carbon charge forms. Known by crooks as "black gold," they are often recovered from store trash bins and the account numbers are used to make purchases against your account. Make sure you ask for, take, and destroy those carbon papers!

154. Police reports: Always contact the local police and file a report if you are robbed or discover that any of your valuables are missing. Request that a copy of the report you file be made available to you before you leave. Insurance claims almost always require a police report, and you'll need a copy to claim a loss on your income tax returns.

155. Lost driver's licenses: Report your lost or stolen driver's license to the Department of Motor Vehicles in your home state as soon as possible. Your local DMV may be able to send you a temporary permit or electronic mail verifying that you have a valid license. Local police may be able to help you in making contact with your DMV.

156. Secret codes/signals when traveling with family or friends: Set up a series of code words and even hand signals that can be used to alert them you are in trouble. It can be as simple as a phrase like "I need a strong coffee," especially if everyone knows that you are *not* a coffee drinker.

157. If your party gets separated: In the event that you and your party get separated during anything from a major demonstration or terrorist attack to a crowded street festival, establish pre-determined meeting locations and times. Adjust the times to check back every thirty minutes, one hour, etc. Notify officials about the separation and have them assist in watching out for missing friends and family members.

8

WOMEN TRAVELERS

In addition to all the travel tips and guides that have been offered for all travelers, the following are some specific tips for business and vacation women travelers:

158. Clean out your purse: Security experts agree that women carry far more items in their purse than are really needed. Not only does they add weight and bulk, but they can slow you through security screening areas.

159. Leave the purse/handbag behind: Unless it's really needed, you're best to leave large handbags and purses back in the hotel room when traveling or walking around in open public areas. If carried, they should be small and compact, with a strap that can be hung around the neck and not draped casually over the shoulder. Keep your bag in the front and with a sweater or coat buttoned over it.

160. Let your valuables go: Women may be statistically more concerned about street crime than men, but women are more hesitant and resistant to turn over purses, handbags, wallets, passports, money, or credit cards to the criminals. If you're robbed on a face-to-face basis, give them whatever they want. If your purse is snatched or grabbed, don't try to hang on to it! Modern thieves working with cars, scooters, and other accomplices can easily hurt you or even drag you out into car traffic if you continue to fight to keep that bag.

161. Walking in public: When out in cities, it's always advisable to walk confidently, head high and at a moderately fast pace. Make it look like you're moving quickly to your next business appointment. Also, it's best to not walk close to the curb. Stay closer to building fronts. A lot of purse-snatchers are now working over victims by riding bicycles and scooters.

Try to walk and stay relatively close to others that are walking in the same direction. You don't have to crowd and join their group, but there is truth in the old saying of "safety in numbers."

162. Avoid the restaurant scams: While men are also victims of scamming restaurateurs, women are more often the prime targets of menus placed outside to entice you in with great dishes at cheap prices—only later to hear that the cost of drinks are doubled, prices were for the lunch menu only, there is a two-drink minimum, and that there are extra service charges and mandatory gratuities. Check the prices before you order anything more than a glass of water.

Street-side and outdoor dining areas along busy streets in any major tourist area may provide great views, but they offer little protection or security while dining. They are open to vehicle and shooting attacks and are often targeted by criminals.

163. Watch out for hidden charges everywhere: Before any financial transaction—from taking a cab to even renting a room—always find out the total charge. Women are often victims of hidden charges and extras, such as a taxi's actual meter reading *plus* gas and tolls, a hotel's extra charge for changing bedsheets, etc.

164. Beware of drinks or meals with strangers: While it's nice to meet and make new friends, having drinks or a meal with a stranger the first time you meet them can be trouble. Reports of train and bus passengers being drugged only to wake up later and find they have been fleeced are all too common.

165. Extra feminine items: Take along a few extra personal items, such as feminine napkins or tampons, wet wipes, birth control pills or contraceptive devices, and STD-preventing condoms!

166. Car safety: At home, and while traveling, get your car keys out of your purse before you get to the car. Have the door key in your hand and ready to go. Look around, under, and inside the car before entering, and always check the backseat. Keep your car in gear when stopped for a light and be ready to sound your horn and race away—even if the light is red—if you feel threatened. If you're alone in the city, always drive with the windows up. Use the heater or the air conditioner!

9

IF YOU BECOME A VICTIM OF A CRIME OR HIJACKING

How would you handle yourself if you became a victim of terrorism, a criminal attack or a hijacking? Keep calm, use your head, and realize you still have some options open to you.

167. Don't panic: Easier said than done, but panic never helped any situation and it could get you in worse trouble. Cool heads are going to prevail.

168. Terrorists will use violence: Up until the 9/11 aircraft hijackings, the prevailing philosophy was that unless you're well trained, armed, and have the opportunity to resist, your chances of survival are much better if you cooperate and turn over your valuables. Today, you, the flight attendant, and your fellow passengers may be the first, last, and best line of defense in taking down a crazy or a terrorist.

If you are on the street or in a building when any sort of attack occurs, it is best to remember three things: 1) Run. 2) Hide. 3) As a last resort, *fight like hell!*

169. Criminals will use violence: Unlike being on an airplane, a bus, a cruise liner, or other high-profile hijack situation, if you are victim of street crime you should give the thugs what they want. Remember faces, clothing, accents, and anything else you might be able to give to the police after the fact. The key is being around to give the information to the authorities after the incident!

170. Terrorists are nervous, too: Many terrorists are first-timers and are equally scared and very nervous. Oftentimes if passengers were a little more alert, the terrorists could have been spotted and foiled before they launched their attack.

171. Hide embarrassing material: Hopefully you have pre-located someplace to use as a stash or hide-away area. If you can, quietly get rid of or hide anything the terrorists might find upsetting. This may include reading material, confidential papers, passports, and even liquor.

172. Watch for additional terrorists: Realize terrorists may show up at varying times after an attack or hijacking has begun. A terrorist may have even planned for additional support to arrive later. Someone sitting next to you could be part of the conspiracy.

173. Always be cooperative: Do not be provocative or antagonistic. Even direct eye contact can be considered a threatening gesture. If questioned by your captors, keep your answers short. Do not offer long explanations. But be ready to react and attack back if the opportunity presents itself.

174. Make mental notes: Pay attention to everything that is happening. How many terrorists are there? What are their intentions?

What do they look like? How are they armed? All that information is going to be extremely valuable to the authorities if you are released or escape.

175. Cell phones: While cell phones may not have been effective against the 9/11 terrorists, they are a valuable modern-day technology tool for travel around the nation and the world. In the event of an emergency . . . use yours!

176. Weapons: Look around your seat, cabin, or area you are being held and see if there is anything you have with you, or what else you might use as a weapon or means of escape if the chance presents itself. A briefcase or seat cushion can be used as a shield; a belt can be used as a hand-wrap/knuckle protector or a pain-giving sling with the buckle; a heavy boot makes a decent sap, a fire extinguisher can be deadly, and even a metal writing pen can be used as a shank.

Needless to say, traveling with any sort of knives or sharp objects onboard airlines or cruise ships, as well as some rail and bus lines, has become much more restrictive. If you need to have something for personal protection, it might be best to purchase these items once you arrive at your destination . . . and give them away or trash them before you plan on returning home.

177. Establish passenger/hostage rapport: Look around and evaluate your fellow passengers or hostages. Who do you think is strong? Who do you think is weak? Can you establish eye contact and secret face-signals with others that are likely to help or assist with resistance or escape? Who could you count on for help? Nervous wrecks should definitely be avoided.

178. Evaluate the possibility of resistance: Is it possible to somehow foil the terrorists? If so, how are you going to do it? What might go wrong? Are additional passengers or hostages going to be needed, and can they be counted upon to help? During the 9/11 attacks, brave heroes on United Airlines Flight 93 resisted and gave their lives to keep terrorists from possibly striking the White House or the Capitol. "Let's roll!" were Todd Beamer's last words to his wife, via one of the plane's seat-back phones, before he led the resistance against the onboard terrorists.

179. Evaluate the possibilities of escape: Even if resistance to the terrorists is out of the question, evaluate the possibilities of escape. Do you know where the building's exits are? If you're on an aircraft, where are the emergency exits, and do you know how to activate the exit doors and the emergency slides?

180. Give up your valuables: Never attempt to keep anything of value that your captors may want—even if it has great sentimental value. Keep your mouth closed and give it to them. If you don't, you have marked yourself as provocative and a possible threat.

181. Your occupation: If you have done your homework and have nothing incriminating on you or in your purse or briefcase, never admit you are a member of the military, an executive for an aerospace company or large corporation, a diplomat, or the like. Try to

For business travelers, all your work badges should either be left at home or packed away in your checked luggage until you arrive at your destination and need them to conduct business. Wearing and flashing your credential badges is a great way to tell terrorists or criminals way too much about who you are what you do for a living.

keep your occupation hidden if at all possible.

182. Sit still and keep quiet: Never make any sudden movements. They could have disastrous results. Keep telling yourself to sit still. Don't ask questions of your captors unless they are willing to talk. Don't try to carry on obvious conversations with other hostages. Never get caught trying to pass notes or other objects to others.

183. Ask permission for everything: This includes taking medication, going to the bathroom, removing your coat, getting a drink of water, and requesting something to eat. Eat whatever is given to you, even if it is unappetizing.

184. Listen to crewmembers: Since the 9/11 attacks, most all of the domestic and international airline and cruise line carriers are giving specific training to their crews on how to respond to a terrorist attack or hijacking. Follow their instructions exactly. If asked to help, do so. It may be up to you to save yourself and other passengers.

185. Passing time: Although it will seem like an eternity, keep in mind that time is on your side. Time that passes without a disaster means that something is happening—possibly negotiations or the mobilization of rescue teams. If your captivity stretches out for a long period of time, establish a daily program and schedule of both mental and physical activity.

186. Hit the deck: If a rescue attempt is made, there is little at that point that you can do to help. *Leave it to the professionals.* Try to get onto the floor between the seats on an airplane, or behind any sort of cover in a building or on the street. Lie perfectly still until all shootings and explosions are over and you are instructed on how to get out and get away.

187. Get out quickly: If a rescue is successful, leave quickly. Do not attempt to take anything with you. It could have been boo-by-trapped, or there could be time-delayed explosives hidden in it. Get out of the plane, boat, or building immediately!

10

TRAVELING WITH CHILDREN

Today, traveling domestically or internationally with children is commonplace. Families are doing more traveling together than ever before, and the days of leaving the kids with the grandparents, have gone by the wayside. While these tips are not terror-specific, they do relate to travel challenges and crimes that everyone, regardless of family size, needs to be aware of.

188. Discounts for young travelers: Oftentimes airlines, hotels, cruise ships, and restaurants offer substantial discounts for young travelers, but you have to ask about them!

189. Infants on airliners: Infants traveling on airliners with parents who are paid passengers can often travel for free as "lap children." While the discounts and savings are obvious, there are major concerns about safety for both the parents and the children. Belting a baby in the lap of a parent can, in the event of a crash, be a death trap. Best bet is to use an infant seat designed for babies up to twenty pounds, and mount the seat to face rearward. Check with the airlines to see if there is a discount for traveling with infants or small children.

190. Toddlers on airliners: Usually after the age of two years old, airliners are going to require you purchase the toddler a ticket for travel. While infant and toddler "car seats" are rarely, if ever, required for travel by airlines, they are one of the best insurance policies you can provide for young travelers. A government-approved child safety restraint system is a hard-backed child safety seat; it provides much greater protection for the infant or toddler (up to forty pounds) than a simple lap belt in a full-size airline seat. For a toddler, mount the seat so that it faces forward. Not all car seats are approved by the Federal Aviation Administration for air travel. Check the child's car seat label to make sure it says "This restraint is certified for use in motor vehicles and aircraft," or look it up by the manufacturer on the Internet. These same seats are also likely to come in handy for travel once you reach your destination for any car, bus, or train travels. Many airlines will actually waive any additional baggage charges for infant seats, breast pumps, and even diapers.

Depending upon the specific airline and their regulations, some will allow infants and small children to still sit on the parent's lap while flying. Others require a child's airline seat or restraint system. A variety of companies manufacture safety harnesses designed for young travelers from one to five years of age and weighing twenty-two to forty-four pounds. Check with your airline about their requirements. Some will even provide/rent you what you need.
Photo courtesy of kidsflysafe.com.

191. Young children on airliners: In days gone by, after the young traveler reached the age of four (and weighed at least forty pounds), they were often put into booster seats. Safety tests indicated these booster chairs were not as safe as originally believed. Best recommendation is for children over forty pounds to be strapped into the airline seat just like any other passenger, or secured with a Child Aviation Restraint System (CARES). A wide variety of makers and models can be found on the Internet.

192. Discuss travel plans and concerns: Talk to your children about their upcoming trip. Tell them all about the wonderful activities you plan on doing together, but also spend time talking about security concerns. Never go with strangers, what to do if they get lost or become separated, how to summon emergency help, and what to do in the event of an emergency.

193. Unescorted young travelers: More and more children—ages five to fourteen—are traveling without family members. Officially it is called the Unaccompanied Minor Program (UM). Most airlines do not report the number of UM travelers, but conservative estimates say that it is in the hundreds of thousands.

Get updated rules and regulations well in advance about airline procedures. Some airlines have a policy of accepting unescorted young travelers on nonstop flights only. Others allow intra-airline plane changes only. Most airlines charge between $40 and $90 each way for escort service, in addition to the airline ticket cost. If two or more children are flying together, the fee is usually charged just once by the airline. These charges include ID badges, airport escort at departure and arrival airport, onboard flight attendant notification, and releasing of the UM to authorized family or friend who *must* show a photo ID.

194. Limit a young traveler's travel money: Don't let young travelers carry large amounts of cash along with them. Not only are they more likely to lose it, but they are often victims of robbery just like any adult. Never give your child a credit card. Chances are excellent that no merchant would accept it anyway. If they are traveling alone to meet and stay with family and friends, wire money ahead.

195. Onboard activities: Spending a few minutes in planning for a long trip on behalf of a child can pay off in maximum benefits. This is the key to keeping them occupied, entertained, and quiet. Most kids, like many adults, have a very limited attention span. Video games, reading books, MP3 players, and even old-fashioned crayons and coloring books should be considered a must.

196. Special meals: Young traveler's taste in airline food is often much fussier and more discriminating than the seasoned traveling adult. If you are on a long enough flight that includes meal service, check with the airlines at least forty-eight hours before departure about special kids' meals that may be available. Judging by some airline cuisine designed for adults, you might even want to order one for yourself!

197. Special snacks: Expecting a young traveler to wait for an hour or more after takeoff to be served a cold drink and a bag of pretzels is often pushing the limit of a child's patience. Have a couple bags of special snacks ready for immediate use. Limit the sweets and candies, and try little bags of cut vegetables, fruit, nuts, granola bars, etc. Most everything you might want can be purchased once you are inside the terminal and past the security checkpoints.

198. Babysitters: Whether on business or vacation, sometimes it's nice to be able to leave the kids behind for a special night out. Cruise ships almost always have infant care centers, babysitters, and plenty of young traveler activities and supervisors. Large hotels domestic and internationally often maintain lists of pre-screened babysitters. Check with the hotel's concierge about these lists, the sitters' ages, qualifications, rates, ages of children, etc. Some hotels have their own certification course for sitters and actually have them bonded. Others, unfortunately, have nothing at all.

199. Ground travel—car seats and frequent breaks: If your children are still in car seats, make use of them with all your ground travels. Many countries have no rules or regulations for travel with infants and toddlers. It's a good safety policy to make sure the children are in safety seats and with lap and shoulder belts, regardless of whether it's required or not.

When traveling with young travelers, expect high levels of "kid's energy," and plan more frequent stops to let them get out and have a little exercise and fun. About ninety minutes of travel time followed by a ten- to fifteen-minute stop is a great way to help keep the peace and add some harmony.

200. Take a current photo of your child with you: In the event your child ends up missing, having an actual paper photo can help everyone from law enforcement to locals identify them and return them quickly. Pics on the cell phone are great, but what if your phone is lost or stolen?

201. Parental notes: Write down the child's name, address, phone number, hotel information and phone, passport number, etc., and have your child keep it with them at all times. In the event of an emergency, children often can forget vital information about themselves. Being able to hand a policeman a note with this information when separated from others is a cheap insurance policy for your children.

It is also a good idea to have a notarized copy of a Travel Consent

Letter if the child is not traveling with both parents. Ideally, this letter should be signed and notarized by both parents. If you are a single parent traveling with a child to an international destination, you may be asked to provide a consent letter by an immigration officer, the airlines, or the travel company.

11

U.S. EMBASSIES AND CONSULATES

While you are traveling abroad, U.S. embassies and consulates are available to help you with all serious medical, legal, and financial problems. They will help you find medical aid and can inform friends and family if you become ill or are injured. They will assist in replacing your lost passport or visa, and can arrange to have emergency funds sent to you by your family, friends, bank, or employer. They can provide lists of local legal counsel, notarize documents and provide U.S. tax forms. They can give you up-to-date information on travel advisories and problem areas where a threat may be high, and they can also give information on absentee voting, as well as the acquisition or loss of U.S. citizenship.

The American Citizens Services (ACS) Unit at the embassy or the consulate is the one that is trained and used to dealing with most problems that travelers from the United States encounter. The ACS cannot act as your travel agent, bank, lawyer, investigator, or law enforcement agent. Please do not expect the office to find you employment, obtain residence or driving permits, act as interpreters or translators, search for missing luggage, or settle disputes with hotel managers.

They cannot act as your legal counsel, but they can advise you of your rights. If you are arrested, they will make sure that you are not held under inhumane conditions. In emergencies, they can even provide you with food and clothing.

The complete list of all embassies and consulates can be obtained by writing to the United States State Department in Washington, DC, or by going to their website at www.usembassy.state.gov.

Prepare yourself for a lot of information overload, as you will have to do a lot of navigating to find specific information about the embassy or consulate, its location, and any specific threats or warnings in the country you plan to travel. A much easier way to wade through all the non-useful information about and get valuable travel data and country specific warnings is to go to http://travel.state.gov/content/passports/en/country.html. Simply type in the name of the country or countries that you plan on visiting and you can instantly find out everything you need to know about passport and visa requirements, vaccinations, currency restrictions, and the latest travel, terror, crime, and safety warnings.

In the old days, worldwide travelers were told to check in upon arrival in a foreign nation with the U.S. embassy or consulate general's office to let them know that you were "in-country," where you were staying and how to contact you in the event of an emergency. Today, U.S. citizens can quickly and easily enroll online with the Department of State using the Smart Traveler Enrollment Program (STEP). This secure website allows U.S. citizens to record foreign trip and residence information so that the Department of State can communicate with you and assist you in case of an emergency.

STEP (https://step.state.gov/step) allows the traveler to register in advance, and update the contact information on the Internet at any time. The site also provides up-to-date travel information customized to any unique travel agenda and itinerary. It also enables the traveler's friends, business associates, and family to receive updated information about the countries you are traveling in. And, if you are not traveling now, but are interested in monitoring safety conditions for specific destination(s) overseas, you can sign up for email alerts to receive the latest Travel Alerts and Warnings when they are posted.

The data you provide is secured behind Department of State firewalls, accessed only by cleared personnel in embassies, consulates, and the Department of State, and releasable only under the provisions of the Privacy Act.

According to the official website:

> Millions of Americans travel abroad every year and encounter no difficulties. However, U.S. embassies and consulates assist nearly 200,000 Americans each year who are victims of crime, accident, or illness, or whose family and friends need to contact them in an emergency. When an emergency happens, or if natural disaster, terrorism, or civil unrest strikes during your foreign travel, the nearest U.S. embassy or consulate can be your source of assistance and information. By informing us about your trip or residence abroad, you help the embassy or consulate locate you when you might need them the most. Signing up is voluntary and costs nothing, but it should be a big part of your travel planning and security.

As of today, there are nearly two hundred countries where you can find U.S. embassies and consulate general offices that are maintained by the U.S. Department of State. Our listing here of embassies and consulate general offices make up the vast majority of the countries and nations that travelers, tourists, and business people are likely to visit. To locate information on other nations that are not listed, simply go to www.state.gov/misc/list/index.htm.

AFGHANISTAN

U.S. Embassy, The Great Masoud (Airport) Road, Kabul, Afghanistan; Telephone: +(93) 0700-108-001 or 002; Fax +(93) 0700-108-564; Email: kabulacs@state.gov

ANGOLA

U.S. Embassy, Rua Houari Boumedienne #32, Luanda, Angola; Telephone: +(244) 222-64-1000; Fax: +(244) 222-64-1232; Email: consularluanda@state.gov

ARGENTINA

U.S. Embassy, Av. Colombia 4300 (C1425GMN) Buenos Aires Argentina; Telephone: +(54-11) 5777-4533; Fax: +(54-11) 5777-4240; Email: BuenosAires-ACS@state.gov

AUSTRALIA

U.S. Consulate General, Level 10, MLC Centre, 19-29 Martin Place, Sydney, NSW 2000, Australia; Telephone: +(61) (2) 4422-2201; Fax: +(61) (2) 9373-9184; Email: SydneyACS@state.gov

AUSTRIA

U.S. Embassy, Boltzmanngasse 16, 1090, Vienna, Austria; Telephone: +(43-1) 31339-0; Fax: +(43-1) 310 06 82; Email: embassy@usembassy.at

THE BAHAMAS

U.S. Embassy, 42 Queen Street, Nassau, The Bahamas; Telephone +(242) 322-1181; Fax: +(242) 356-7174; Email: acsnassau@state.gov

BARBADOS/EASTERN CARIBBEAN

U.S. Embassy, Alico Building, Cheapside, Bridgetown, Barbados,

West Indies; Telephone: +(246) 227-4000; Fax: +(246) 431-0179; Email: bridgetownacs@state.gov

BELGIUM
U.S. Embassy, Regentlaan 27 Boulevard du Regent, B-1000, Brussels, Belgium; Telephone: +(32-2) 811-4000; Fax: +(32-2) 811-4500; Email: ic@usinfo.be

BELIZE
U.S. Embassy, 4 Floral Park Road, Belmopan, Belize; Telephone: +(501) 822-4011; Fax: +(501) 822-4050; Email: ACSBelize@state.gov

BERMUDA
U.S. Consulate General, Crown Hill, 16 Middle Road, Devonshire DV03, Bermuda; Telephone: +(441) 295-1342; Fax: +(441) 295-1592; Email: HamiltonConsulate@state.gov

BOLIVIA
U.S. Embassy, Avenida Arce #2780, La Paz, Bolivia; Telephone: +(591-2) 216-8246; Fax: +(591-2) 216-8808; Email: Consular-LaPazACS@state.gov

BOSNIA AND HERZEGOVINA
U.S. Embassy, 1 Robert C. Frasure Street, 71000 Sarajevo, Bosnia and Herzegovina; Telephone: +(387) 33 704-000; Fax +(387) 33 221-837; Email: SarajevoACS@state.gov

BOTSWANA
U.S. Embassy, Embassy Drive, Government Enclave, Gaborone, Botswana; Telephone: +(267) 373-2201; Fax: +(267) 318-0232; Email: ConsularGaborone@State.Gov

BRAZIL

U.S. Embassy, SES 801- Avenida Das Nacoes, Lote 03, 70403-900-Brasilia, DF Brazil; Telephone: +(55) (61) 312-7000; Fax: +(55) (61) 312-7651; Email: BrasiliaACS@state.gov

CAMEROON

U.S Embassy, Avenue Rosa Parks, P.O. Box 817, Yaounde, Cameroon; Telephone: +(237) 22220-15-00; Fax: +(237) 22220-15-72; Email: YaoundeACS@state.gov

CANADA

U.S. Embassy, 490 Sussex Drive, K1N 1G8, Ottawa, Ontario, Canada; Telephone: 613-238-5335; Fax: 613-688-3082; Email: ottawaACS@state.gov

CHILE

U.S. Embassy, Av. Andres Bello 2800, Las Condes, Santiago, Chile; Telephone: +(56-2) 2330-3000; Fax: +(562) 2330-3710; Email: santiagoamcit@state.gov

CHINA

U.S. Embassy, 55 An Jia Lou Lu 100600, Beijing, China; Telephone: +(86-10) 8531-4000; Fax: +(86-10) 8531-3300; Email: BeijingACS@state.gov

COLOMBIA

U.S. Embassy, Calle 24 Bis No. 48-50 Bogotá, D.C. Colombia; Telephone: +(571) 275 2000; Fax: +(571) 275 4501; Email: ACSBogota@state.gov

COSTA RICA

U.S. Embassy, Calle 98, Via 104, Pavas, Costa Rica; Telephone:

+(506) 2519-2000; Fax: +(506) 2200-2455; Email: acssanjose@ state.gov

CROATIA

U.S. Embassy, Ulica Thomasa Jeffersona 2. 10010 Zagreb, Croatia; Telephone: +(385) (1) 661-2200; Fax +(385) (1) 665-8933; Email: ZagrebACS@state.gov

CUBA

U.S. Embassy, Calzada between L and M Streets, Vedado, Havana, Cuba; Telephone: +(53) (7) 839-4100; Fax +(53) (7) 839-4247; Email: ACSHavana@state.gov

CYPRUS

U.S. Embassy, Metochiou & Ploutarchou Street, 2407, Engomi, Nicosia, Cyprus; Telephone: +(357) 2239-3939; Fax: +(357) 2239-3344; Email: consularnicosia@state.gov

CZECH REPUBLIC

U.S. Embassy, Trziste 15, 118 01 Praha 1, Mala Strana, Czech Republic; Telephone: +(420) 257 022 000; Fax: +(420) 257-022-809; Email: ACSPrg@state.gov

DEMOCRATIC REPUBLIC OF THE CONGO

U.S. Embassy. 310, Avenue des Aviateurs, Kinshasa, Gombe, Democratic Republic of the Congo; Telephone: +(243) 081-556-0151; Fax: +(243) 081-556-0169; Email: AEKinshasaConsular@state.gov

DENMARK

U.S. Embassy, Dag Hammarskjolds Alle 24, 2100, Copenhagen, Denmark; Telephone: +(45) 3341-7100; Fax +(45) 3538-9616; Email: copenhagenACS@state.gov

DOMINICAN REPUBLIC

U.S. Embassy, Av. República de Colombia #57, Santo Domingo, Dominican Republic; Telephone +(809) 567-7775; Fax: none; Email: SDOAmericans@state.gov

EGYPT

U.S. Embassy, Consular Section, 5 Tawfik Diab Street, Garden City, Cairo, Egypt; Telephone: +(20) 2797-3300; Fax: +(20) 2797-2472; Email: consularcairoacs@state.gov

EL SALVADOR

U.S. Embassy, Boulevard Santa Elena, Antiguo Cuscatlan, La Libertad, El Salvador; Telephone: +(503) 2501-2999; Fax: +(503) 2278-5522; Email: acssansal@state.gov or CongenSansal@state.gov

ETHIOPIA

U.S. Embassy, Entoto Street, PO Box 1014, Addis Ababa, Ethiopia; Telephone: + (251) 11-130-6000; Fax: +(251) 11-124-2435; Email: consacs@state.gov

FINLAND

U.S. Embassy, Itaiinen Puistotie 14 B, 00140 Helsinki, Finland; Telephone: +(358) 9-616-250; Fax: +(358) 9-174-681; Email: HelsinkiACS@state.gov

FRANCE

U.S. Embassy, 2 Avenue Gabriel, 75382, Paris, France; Telephone: +(33) (1) 43-12-22-22; Fax +(33) (1) 42-66-97-83; Email: Citizeninfo@state.gov

GERMANY

U.S. Embassy, Clayallee 170, 14191 Berlin, Germany; Telephone:

+(49) 30-8305-0; Fax: +(49) 30-8305-1215; Email: ACSBerlin@
state.gov

GREECE
U.S. Embassy, 91 Vassillisis Sophis Ave., Athens 10160, Greece;
Telephone: +(30) 210-720-2414; Fax: +(30) 210-724-5313;
Email: athensamericancitizenservices@state.gov

GUATEMALA
U.S. Embassy, Avenida Refmora 7-01, Zona 10, Guatemala City,
Guatemala; Telephone: +(502) 2326-4000; Fax: +(502) 2331-
3804; Email: AmCitsGuatemala@state.gov

HAITI
U.S. Embassy, Boulevard du 15 October, Tabarre 41, Route de
Tabarre, Port-au-Prince, Haiti; Telephone: +(509) 2229-8000;
Fax: +(509) 2229-8027; Email: acspap@state.gov

HONDURAS
U.S. Embassy, Avenida La Paz. Tegucigalpa M.D.C., Honduras;
Telephone: +(504) 2236-9320; Fax: +(504) 2236-9037; Email:
usahonduras@state.gov

HONG KONG
U.S. Consulate General, 26 Garden Road, Central, Hong Kong;
Telephone: +(852) 2841-2211; Fax: +(852) 2845-4845; Email:
acshk@state.gov

HUNGARY
U.S. Embassy, Szabadsag ter 12, H-1054 Budapest, Hungary; Telephone: +(36) (1) 475-4400; Fax: +(36) (1) 475-4188; Email: acs.
budapest@state.gov

ICELAND
U.S. Embassy, Laufásvegur 21, 101 Reykjavik, Iceland; Telephone: +(354) 595-2200; Fax: +(354) 562-9118; Email: ReykjavikConsular@state.gov

INDIA
U.S. Embassy, Shantipath, Chanakyapuri, New Delhi-1100021, India; Telephone: +(91) (11) 2419-8000; Fax: +(91) (11) 2419-8407; Email: newdelghi@pd.state.gov

INDONESIA
U.S Embassy, Jl. Medan Merdeka Selatan No. 3 - 5, Jakarta 10110, Indonesia; Telephone: +(62) (21) 3435-9000; Fax: +(62) (21) 385-7189; Email: jakconsul@state.gov

IRAQ
U.S. Embassy, Al-Kindi Street, International Zone; Baghdad, Iraq; Telephone: +(964) 770-443-1286; Fax: none; Email: baghdad-acs@state.gov

IRELAND
U.S. Embassy, 42 Elgin Road Ballsbridge, Dublin 4, Ireland; Telephone: +(353) (1) 668-8777; Fax: +(353) (1) 668-9946; Email: ascdublin@state.gov

ISRAEL
U.S. Embassy, 71 Hayarkon Street, Tel Aviv, Israel, 63903; Telephone: +(972) (3) 519-7575; Fax: +(972) (3) 516-4390; Email: amctelaviv@state.gov

ITALY
U.S. Embassy, Via Vittorio Veneto, 121, 00187 Rome, Italy; Tele-

phone: +(39) 06-46741; Fax: +(39) 06-4674-2217; Email: uscitizensrome@state.gov

JAMAICA
U.S. Embassy, 142 Old Hope Road, Kingston 6, Jamaica, West Indies; Telephone: +(876) 702-6000; Fax: +(876) 702-6018; Email: KingstonACS@state.gov

JAPAN
U.S. Embassy, 1-10-5 Akasaka, Minato-ku, Tokyo, 107-8420, Japan; Telephone: +(81) (3) 3224-5000; Fax: +(81) (3) 3224-5856; Email: Tokyoacs@state.gov

JORDAN
U.S. Embassy, Al-Umayyaween Street, Abdoun neighborhood, Amman 11118, Jordan; Telephone: +(962) (6) 590-6000; Fax: +(962) (6) 592-4102; Email: Amman-ACS@state.gov

KENYA
U.S. Embassy, United Nations Avenue, Gigiri, Nairobi, Kenya; Telephone +(254) (20) 363-6451; Fax: +(254) (20) 363-6501; Email: kenya_acs@state.gov

KUWAIT
U.S. Embassy, Bayan, Block 13, Masjed Al-Aqsa Street, Kuwait City, Kuwait; Telephone: +(965) 2259-1001; Fax: +(965) 2259-1438; Email: kuwaitACS@state.gov

LEBANON
U.S. Embassy, Jemil Street, Awkar; Beruit, Lebanon; Telephone: +(961) 4-542600: Fax +(961) 4-544209; Email: BeirutACS@state.gov

MALAYSIA

U.S. Embassy, 376 Jalan Tun Razak, 50400, Kuala Lumpur, Malaysia; Telephone: +(60) (3) 2168-4997; Fax: +(60) (3) 2148-5801; Email: klacs@state.gov

MEXICO

U.S. Embassy, Paseo de la Reforma 305, Colonia Cuauhtemoc Mexico, D.F. Mexico C.P. 06500; Telephone: +(52) (55) 5080-2000; Fax: +(52) (55) 5080-2201; Email: acsmexicocity@state.gov

MOROCCO

U.S. Consulate General, 8, Bd Moulay Youssef, Casablanca, Morocco; Telephone: +(212) (522) 26-45-50; Fax: +(212) (522) 20-80-97; Email: acscasablanca@state.gov

MOZAMBIQUE

U.S. Embassy, Avenida Kenneth Kaunda, 193, Maputo, Mozambique; Telephone: +(258) 21-49-2797; Fax: +(258) 21-49-0448; Email: consularmaputo@state.gov

NAMIBIA

U.S. Embassy, 14 Lossen Street, Ausspannplatz, Windhoek, Namibia; Telephone: +(264) (61) 295-8522; Fax: +(264) (61) 295-8603; Email: consularwindho@state.gov

NEPAL

U.S. Embassy, Maharajgunj, Kathmandu, Nepal; Telephone: +(977) (1) 423-4500; Fax: +(977) (1) 400-7281; Email: consktm@state.gov

NETHERLANDS (Holland)

U.S. Embassy, Museumplein 19, 1071 DJ, Amsterdam, Netherlands; Telephone: +(31) (20) 575-5309; Fax: +(31) (0) 20-575-5330; Email: USCitizenServicesAms@state.gov

NEW ZEALAND

U.S Consulate General, 3rd Floor, Citigroup Building, 23 Customs Street East (cnr. Commerce St), Auckland, New Zealand; Telephone: +(64) (9) 303-2724; Fax: +(64) (9) 366-0870; Email: aucklandacs@state.gov

NICARAGUA

U.S. Embassy, Km 5 1/2 (5.5) Carretera Sur, Managua, Nicaragua; Telephone: +(505) 2252-7100; Fax: +(505) 2252-7250; Email: acs.managua@state.gov

NIGERIA

U.S. Embassy, 1075 Diplomatic Drive Central District Area, Abuja, Nigeria; Telephone: +(234) 9-461-4000 Fax: +(234) 9-461-4171; Email: Consularabuja@state.gov

NORWAY

U.S. Embassy, Henrik Ibsens gate 48, 0244 Oslo, Norway; Telephone: +(47) 2130-8787; Fax +(47) 2256-2751; Email: osloacs@state.gov

PAKISTAN

U.S. Embassy, Diplomatic Enclave, Ramna 5, Islamabad, Pakistan; Telephone: +(92) (51) 204-0000; Fax: +(92) (51) 282-2632; Email: ACSIslamabad@state.gov

PANAMA

U.S. Embassy, Avenida Demetrio Basilio Lakas, Building No.783, Clayton, Panama; Telephone: +(507)-317-5000; Fax: +(507) 317-5568; Email: Panama-ACS@state.gov

PERU

U.S. Embassy, Avenida Encalada, Cdra 17 sn, Surco, Lima, Peru; Telephone: +(51) (1) 618-2000; Fax: +(51) (1) 618-2724; Email: LimaACS@state.gov

PHILIPPINES

U.S. Embassy, 1201 Roxas Blvd, 1 Manila, Philippines, 1000; Telephone: +(63) (2) 301-2000; Fax: +(63) (2) 301-2017; Email: acsinfomanila@state.gov

POLAND

U.S. Embassy, Aleje Ujazdowskie 29/31, 00-540 Warsaw, Poland; Telephone: +48 (22) 504-2000; American Citizen Services: +(48) (22) 504-2784; Fax: +(48) (22) 504-2122; Email: acswarsaw@state.gov

PORTUGAL

U.S. Embassy, Av. Das Forças Armadas, Sete-Rios, 1600-081, Lisbon, Portugal; Telephone: +(351) (21) 770-2122; Fax: +(351) (21) 727-2354; Email: conslisbon@state.gov

QATAR

U.S. Embassy, Al Luqta District, 22nd February Street, P.O. Box 2399, Doha, Qatar; Telephone: +(974) 4496-6000; Fax: +(974) 4488-4298; Email: acsconsulardoha@state.gov

ROMANIA

U.S. Embassy, B-dul Dr. Liviu Librescu Nr. 4-6, Sector 1, Bucharest, 015118 Romania; Telephone: +(40) (21) 200-3300; Fax: +(40) (21) 200-3578; Email: ACSBucharest@state.gov

RUSSIA

U.S. Embassy, Bolshoy Devyatinskiy Pereulok No. 8, Moscow

122099, Russian Federation; Telephone: +(7) (495) 728-5000; Fax: +(7) (495) 728-5084; Email: moscowwarden@state.gov

SAUDI ARABIA

U.S. Embassy, Abdullah Ibn Hudhafah As Sahmi Street, Roundabout no. 9, Diplomatic Quarter, Riyadh, Saudi Arabia; Telephone: +(966) (11) 488-3800; Fax: +(966) (11) 488-7670; Email: RiyadhACS@state.gov

SINGAPORE

U.S. Embassy, 27 Napier Road, Singapore 258508; Telephone: +(65) 6476-9100; Fax: +(65) 6476-9232; Email: singaporeacs@state.gov

SOUTH AFRICA

U.S. Consulate General, 1 Sandton Drive, Johannesburg 2196, South Africa; Telephone: +(27) (11) 290-3000; Fax: +(27) (11) 884-0396; Email: consularjohannesburg@state.gov

SOUTH KOREA

U.S. Embassy, in Seoul, Korea 188 Sejong-daero, Jongno-gu, Seoul, Republic of Korea, 110-710; Telephone: +(82) (2) 397-4114; Fax: +(82) (2) 397-4101; Email: seoulinfoACS@state.gov

SPAIN

U.S. Embassy, Calle Serrano 75, 28006 Madrid, Spain; Telephone: +(34) (91) 587-2200; Fax: +(34) (91) 587-2303; Email: askacs@state.gov

SUDAN

U.S. Embassy, Kilo 10, Soba, Khartoum, Sudan; Telephone: +(249) 1-870-22000; Fax: none; Email: ACSKhartoum@state.gov

SWEDEN

U.S. Embassy, Dag Hammarskjolds Vag 31, SE-115 89 Stockholm, Sweden; Telephone: +(46) (8) 783-5300; Fax: +(46) (8) 783-5480; Email: stkacsinfo@state.gov

SWITZERLAND

U.S. Embassy, Sulgeneckstrasse 19 3007 Bern, Switzerland; Telephone: +(41) (31) 357-7777; Fax: +(41) (31) 357-7280; Email: bernacs@state.gov

TAIWAN

American Institute in Taiwan, 3rd Floor, Consular Section #7, Lane 134, Hsin Yi Road Section 3, Taipei, 106 Taiwan; Telephone: +(886) 2-2162-2000; Fax: +(886) 2-2162-2239; Email: amcit-ait-t@state.gov

TANZANIA

U.S. Embassy, 686 Old Bagamoyo Road, Msasani, Dar es Salaam, Tanzania; Telephone: + (255) 22-229-4122; Fax: + (255) 22-229-4721; Email: drsacs@state.gov

THAILAND

U.S. Embassy, 95 Wireless Road, Bangkok 10330, Thailand; Telephone: +(66) (2) 205-4049; Fax: +(66) (2) 205-4103; Email: acsbkk@state.gov

TURKEY

U.S. Embassy, 110 Atatürk Blvd., Kavaklidere, 06100 Ankara, Turkey; Telephone: +(90) (312) 455-5555; Fax: +(90) (312) 466-5684; Email: via webpage at https://tr.usembassy.gov/u-s-citizen-services/contact-acs-ankara/

UGANDA

U.S. Embassy, Plot 1577 Ggaba Road, P.O. Box 7007, Kampala,

Uganda; Telephone: +(256) (0) 414-306-001; Fax: none; Email: KampalaUSCitizen@state.gov

UNITED ARAB EMIRATES

U.S. Embassy, Embassies District, Plot 38, Sector W59-02, Street No. 4, Abu Dhabi, United Arab Emirates; Telephone: +(971) (2) 414-2200; Fax: +(971) (2) 414-2241; Email: abudhabiacs@state.gov

UNITED KINGDOM (England, Wales, Scotland, Northern Ireland)

U.S. Embassy, 24 Grosvenor Square, London, W1A 1AE, United Kingdom; Telephone: +(44) (20) 7499-9000; Fax: +(44) (20) 7495-5012; Email: SCSLondon@state.gov

VENEZUELA

U.S. Embassy, Calle F con Calle Suaprre, Urb. Colinas de Valle Arriba, Caracas, Venezuela, 1080; Telephone: +(58) (212) 975-6411; Fax: +(58) (212) 907-8199; Email: ACSVenezuela@state.gov

VIETNAM

U.S. Embassy, 170 Ngoc Khanh Street, Ba Dinh District, Hanoi, Vietnam; Telephone: +(84) (4) 3850-5000; Fax: +(84) (4) 3850-5010; Email: acshanoi@state.gov

ZAMBIA

U.S. Embassy, Eastern end of Kabulonga Road, Ibex Hill, Lusaka, Zambia; Telephone: +(260) 211-357-000; Fax: +(260) (0) 211-357-224; Email: ACSLusaka@state.gov

ZIMBABWE

U.S. Embassy, 172 Herbert Chitepo Avenue, Harare, Zimbabwe; Telephone: +(263) (4) 250-593; Fax: +(263) (4) 250-343; Email: consularharare@state.gov

12

EMERGENCY ASSISTANCE AND MEDICAL AID

Getting ill or injured while at home is no fun. Becoming ill or injured while traveling, especially while overseas, can be a lot worse! Being prepared in advance for domestic travel here in the United States is often as simple as knowing how to dial 911 and request emergency help. When traveling overseas, it can become a lot more complicated.

If an American citizen becomes seriously ill or injured abroad, a U.S. consular officer can assist in locating appropriate medical services and informing family or friends. If necessary a consular officer can also assist in the transfer of funds from the United States. However, payment of hospital and other expenses is the responsibility of the traveler.

Before going abroad, learn what medical services your health insurance will cover while traveling. If your health insurance policy provides coverage outside the United States, *remember to carry both your insurance policy ID card as proof of such insurance and a claim form.* Although many health insurance companies will pay for "customary and reasonable" doctor and hospital costs abroad, very few will pay for your medical evacuation back to the United States if needed. Medical evacuation can easily cost $10,000 or more, depending on your location and medical condition.

Remember also that Social Security Medicare programs do *not* provide coverage for hospital or medical costs outside the United States. Senior citizens may want to contact the American Association of Retired Persons (AARP) at their website of www.aarp.org.

The organization known as the International Association for Medical Assistance to Travellers (IAMAT) was established in 1960 and has participating physicians, specialists, clinics, and hospitals in 125 counties that are staffed with English- or French-speaking physicians who are on call twenty-four hours a day. They publish an annual directory of these medical resources and provide the traveler with the names and addresses of physicians who have agreed to a set payment schedule for a member's first visit.

Although a donation to IAMAT for this most valuable service is requested and appreciated, there is no cost to join, or annual fees to join. Membership is valid for one year and renewable with a donation. Information and sign-up is available on line at www.iamat.org or by calling 716-754- 4883.

To get the latest travel health advisories around the world, begin with the U.S. Centers for Disease Control and Prevention. Their website at http://wwwnc.cdc.gov/travel has all the latest warnings, alerts, and suggested inoculations.

Travelers going abroad with a preexisting medical condition should carry a letter from their personal physician, describing the medical condition and any prescription medications, including the generic name of prescribed drugs.

13

U.S. CUSTOMS AND BORDER PROTECTION

About a million people enter the United States on a daily basis. And each and every one of them arriving at any port of entry is subject to inspection by Customs and Border Protection (CBP) officers for compliance with immigration, customs, and agriculture regulations. Check out their website at http://www.cbp.gov/travel/us-citizens for lots of information about traveling abroad, including regulations and a host of dos and don'ts.

Remember that you may bring into or take out of the country, including by mail, as much money as you wish. However, if it is more than $10,000, you will need to report it to CBP. Ask the CBP officer for the Currency Reporting Form (FinCen 105). The penalties for noncompliance can be severe. And "money" means any monetary instruments and includes U.S. or foreign coins currently in circulation, currency, travelers' checks, money orders, and negotiable instruments or investment securities in bearer form.

Register before you go: Register expensive items such as jewelry, sporting goods, computers, and cameras before you go. Before you leave most U.S. international airports and ports, ask for, fill out, and submit the CBP Form 4457. This form is available from U.S. Customs and Border Protection personnel. You will likely have to show the declared articles when you go through the CBP checkpoint, as well as when you return to the United States. This way, you will not have to pay a customs duty on the items you already own and are traveling with.

Making a declaration: All items you purchased or and are carrying with you upon return to the United States, including gifts purchased or received, have to be declared. While there are a million rules and regulations about values, duties, tax, etc., the general rule of thumb is that your purchased items with a value of up to $800 will be duty free. After that, you will pay a duty that is determined by the Harmonized Tariff System (HTS) that provides duty rates for virtually every item that exists. The HTS is a reference manual that is the size of an unabridged dictionary. With your declaration, plan on showing all your receipts. Try to pack the things you'll need to declare separately.

Duty-free shops: The term "duty-free shop" confuses many travelers. Travelers often think that what they buy in a duty-free shop will not be dutiable when they return home. *This is not true!* Articles sold in a duty-free shop are meant to be taken out of the country, and are dutiable when brought into another country—including the United States.

If you are a frequent traveler, you may want to check out and apply for the CBP's Trusted Traveler Programs, which provide expedited travel for pre-approved, low-risk travelers through dedicated lanes and kiosks. Additional information and application forms are on the CBP's site at http://www.cbp.gov/travel/trusted-traveler-programs.

14

GOVERNMENT SECURITY, SCREENING, AND NO-FLY LISTS

If you think that government security and screening begins once you get to the airport and head for those long TSA security checkpoints, think again! For the fact is, many security screening procedures are now activated the minute you make a reservation on any airline that is operating here in the United States. So . . . who are the wizards behind the secret curtains?

The instant you make a telephone, in-person, or Internet reservation for any flight (domestic or international) the security procedures begin. Once you key in your name, address, gender, date of birth, phone numbers, and payment information on how you are going to pay for the flight. That basic information is used to trigger a background check under a program that the government has used for years and has been called Secure Flight. Unofficially, the information was used and compared to known terrorist watch lists.

Officially, and direct from the Transportation Security Administration (TSA) website (https://www.tsa.gov/travel/security-screening):

Secure Flight is a risk-based passenger prescreening program that enhances security by identifying low and high-risk passengers before they arrive at the airport by matching their names against trusted traveler lists and watchlists.

To protect privacy, the Secure Flight program collects the minimum amount of personal information, such as full name, date of birth, and gender, necessary to conduct effective matching. Read the Privacy Impact Assessment and the System of Records Notice for information about the program's rigorous privacy protections. Personal data is collected, used, distributed, stored and disposed of according to stringent guidelines.

Secure Flight transmits the screening instructions back to the airlines to identify low-risk passengers eligible for TSA Pre√*; individuals on the Selectee List who are designated for enhanced screening; and those who will receive standard screening. Secure Flight also prevents individuals on the No Fly List and Centers for Disease Control and Prevention Do Not Board List from boarding an aircraft. The Travel Redress Program provides resolution for travel-related screening or inspection issues.

If everything checked out and you were considered a "low-risk" traveler, the reservation goes through and allows you to print out your boarding pass while at home or the office.

Now, and since 2013, your basic reservation input can swing to the other extreme, and trigger governmental and private databases to provide much more information about you than you might have ever imagined. Information on your vehicle registrations, employment information, tax identification information, past travel itineraries, passport information, property records, and law enforcement/intelligence databases are all accessible if TSA feels the need.

If you are able to make a reservation and print your boarding pass while finishing your travel plans, chances are excellent that you are not on anyone's "naughty list"! If you can't . . . you may have serious travel problems, headaches, and challenges ahead!

Here again is the official language from the U.S. Department of Homeland Security (DHS) website (https://www.dhs.gov/dhs-trip) and what they call their Traveler Redress Inquiry Program (TRIP)—a program that, in theory, can provide assistance with travel/security woes:

DHS TRIP can help you work to resolve travel-related issues. This applies when:

- You were not able to print a boarding pass from an airline ticketing kiosk or from the Internet
- You were denied or delayed boarding
- A ticket agent "called someone" before handing you a boarding pass
- **You were told:**
  o your fingerprints were incorrect or of poor quality
  o your photo did not match the travel document
  o your personal information was incomplete or inaccurate
  o you are on the "No Fly List"
- **You want to:**
  o amend a traveler record because of an overstay as a result of not submitting the required I-94 when exiting the United States
  o ensure your biometric record in the Department of Homeland Security Systems is corrected if inaccurate.
- **You believe:**
  o you were unfairly detained during your travel experience or unfairly denied entry into the United States
  o the U.S. government's record of your personal information is inaccurate.

Think that all sounds pretty simple and straightforward? Once more, think again. . . .

The Infamous No-Fly List

The No-Fly List is a small subset of the U.S. government's Terrorist Screening Database (also known as the terrorist watchlist) that contains the identity information of known or suspected terrorists. This database is maintained by the FBI's Terrorist Screening Center (TSC). For more information about the Terrorist Screening Database, you can visit the FBI Terrorist Screening Center at https://www.fbi.gov/about-us/nsb/tsc. Individuals on the No-Fly List are prevented from boarding an aircraft when flying within, to, from, and over the United States.

So, who decides who is put on these terror watchlists?

Before the September 11, 2001 attacks, more than a dozen watch lists were floating around all the different federal agencies. Now, all of these records have been consolidated into one master list maintained by the FBI's Terrorist Screening Center.

The development of TSC and today's master list grew out of Homeland Security Presidential Directive 6 signed by President Bush in 2003. The directive outlined the federal government's plan to pull together and combine all former watch lists into one master list of people "known or appropriately suspected to be or have been engaged in conduct constituting, in preparation for, in aid of, or related to terrorism." Exact number of individuals on the No-Fly List is a closely guarded secret, but back in 2013, it was reported to be upward of 47,000 people. As many as 1,200 of these people are American citizens.

By comparison, the Canadian government also maintains a No-Fly List as part of a program called Passenger Protect. It too is a compilation of data that have been gathered from domestic and foreign nation intelligence sources. Information at the disposal of the Canadian government includes the U.S. No-Fly List data. It is believed that the Canadian list contains between five hundred and two thousand names.

Here is the official explanation about what the Terrorist Screening Center does, according to the FBI website, as of April 2016:

• WHAT IS THE TERRORIST SCREENING CENTER AND WHAT DOES IT DO?

The Terrorist Screening Center was established in 2003, pursuant to Presidential Directive, by the Attorney General and is administered by the Federal Bureau of Investigation (FBI). Terrorist Screening Center personnel come from various U.S. Government departments/agencies and are responsible for law enforcement, homeland security, and intelligence operations. The Terrorist Screening Center maintains the Terrorist Screening Database (TSDB), the U.S. Government's consolidated database of identity information about individuals known or reasonably suspected to be or have been engaged in terrorism or terrorist activities.

• WHAT IS THE TERRORIST SCREENING DATABASE AND HOW IS IT USED?

The Terrorist Screening Database (TSDB) is the U.S. Government's consolidated database containing the identity information of known or suspected terrorists. The Terrorist Screening Center shares, as appropriate, information from the Terrorist Screening Database with government agencies that conduct terrorism screening and serves as a bridge between the law enforcement, homeland security, and the intelligence communities, as well as select international partners.

• WHAT IS THE DIFFERENCE BETWEEN THE TERRORIST SCREENING CENTER AND THE NATIONAL COUNTERTERRORISM CENTER?

The Terrorist Screening Center is responsible for maintaining the Terrorist Screening Database and has primary U.S. Government responsibilities for watchlisting known or suspected terrorists, screening, and information sharing. The Terrorist Screening Center is also responsible for sharing information from the Terrorist Screening Database with local, state, federal, tribal, and international partners. The National Counterterrorism Center maintains the Terrorist Identities Datamart Environment which is the U.S. Government's classified central and shared repository for all known or suspected international terrorists and their networks of contacts and support. Certain identities from the Terrorist Identities Datamart Environment are provided to the Terrorist Screening Center for inclusion in the Terrorist Screening Database.

• WHY DO WE HAVE THE TERRORIST SCREENING DATABASE?

The 9/11 Commission Report found that agencies neither shared terrorism information in an effective and timely manner nor appropriately watchlisted terrorists. Through the Terrorist Screening Database, however, the Terrorist Screening Center ensures the timely dissemination of terrorist identity information to its partners who conduct terrorist screening, such as the Department of State, U.S. Customs and Border Protection, and the Transportation Security Administration.

• HOW ARE PEOPLE ADDED TO THE TERRORIST SCREENING DATABASE?

The procedures for submitting terrorist identity information for inclusion in the Terrorist Screening Database are known as the watchlist nomination process. U.S. Government agencies nominate individuals who may qualify for inclusion as a known or suspected terrorist based on credible information and intelligence developed by law enforcement, homeland security, and intelligence community agencies, as well as U.S. Embassies and Consulates.

• WHAT IS THE STANDARD FOR INCLUDING IN-FORMATION IN THE TERRORIST SCREENING DATABASE?

An individual is included in the Terrorist Screening Database when there is a reasonable suspicion that the person is a known or suspected terrorist. To meet the reasonable suspicion standard, nominating agencies must rely upon articulable intelligence or information which taken together with rational inferences from those facts, reasonably warrants a determination that an individual is known or suspected to be or have been knowingly engaged in conduct constituting, in preparation for, in aid of, or related to terrorism or terrorist activities. Based on the totality of the circumstances, a nominating agency must provide an objective factual basis to believe an individual is a known or suspected terrorist.

• WHAT IS THE DEFINITION OF A KNOWN OR SUS-PECTED TERRORIST?

A "known terrorist" is an individual whom the U.S. Government knows is engaged, has been engaged, or who intends to engage in terrorism and/or terrorist activity, including an individual (a) who has been charged, arrested, indicted, or convicted for a crime related to terrorism by U.S. Government or foreign government authorities; or (b) identified as a terrorist or member of a designated foreign terrorist organization pursuant to statute, Executive Order or international legal obligation pursuant to a United Nations Security Council Resolution. A "suspected terrorist" is an individual who is reasonably suspected to be, or has been, engaged in conduct constituting, in preparation for, in aid of, or related to terrorism and/or terrorist activities based on an articulable and reasonable suspicion.

• WHO MAKES THE DECISION TO INCLUDE NAMES IN THE TERRORIST SCREENING DATABASE?

Several layers of review by various U.S. Government agencies occur before a name is added to the Terrorist Screening Database by the Terrorist Screening Center. Agencies submit nominations to the National Counterterrorism Center, which reviews the derogatory information to determine if the provided intelligence forms a sufficient factual basis to reasonably suspect that the person is a known or suspected terrorist. If it does, and if sufficient identifying information is available, the nomination is entered into the Terrorist Identities Datamart Environment (TIDE) and the identifying information is passed to the Terrorist Screening Center for inclusion in the Terrorist Screening Database. The Terrorist Screening Center conducts another review of the nomination and the provided intelligence to verify that the reasonable suspicion standard is met before accepting the record into the Terrorist Screening Database.

• WHAT IS DONE TO ENSURE THE INFORMATION IN THE TERRORIST SCREENING DATABASE IS ACCURATE?

A range of quality control measures are used to ensure that the Terrorist Screening Database contains accurate and timely information. This includes regular reviews, periodic audits, and post-encounter reviews conducted by the Terrorist Screening Center and the agencies that nominated the record to ensure the information continues to satisfy the applicable criteria for inclusion.

• WHICH AGENCIES IN THE UNITED STATES HAVE ACCESS TO THE INFORMATION IN THE TERRORIST SCREENING DATABASE?

Agencies and officials who are authorized to conduct terrorist screening in the course of their official duties have access to the information contained in the Terrorist Screening Database to support diplomatic, military, intelligence, law enforcement, immigration, visa, and protective processes. The five major U.S. Government agencies that screen with information from the Terrorist Screening Database are: the Department of State's consular officers for passport and visa screening; the Transportation Security Administration for aviation security screening (No Fly and Selectee Lists); the FBI's National Crime and Information Center for domestic law enforcement screening; the U.S. Customs and Border Protection for border and port of entry screening; and the Department of Defense for base access screening. All screening functions are subject to U.S. laws and regulations protecting privacy and civil liberties.

• WHAT IS THE NO FLY LIST?

The No Fly List is a subset of the Terrorist Screening Database. Inclusion on the No Fly List prohibits an individual who may present a threat to civil aviation or national security from boarding a commercial aircraft that will fly into, out of, over, or within United States airspace; this also includes point-to-point international flights operated by U.S. carriers. Before an individual may be placed on the No Fly List, there must be credible information that demonstrates the individual poses a threat of committing a violent act of terrorism with respect to civil aviation, the homeland, United States interests located abroad, or is operationally capable of doing so.

• WHAT IS AN "ENCOUNTER"?

An encounter is an event where an individual is identified during a screening process as someone who is a potential match to an identity in the Terrorist Screening Database. For example, an encounter can occur when an individual attempts to board an aircraft, applies for a passport or visa, presents at a U.S. port of entry, or has an interaction with law enforcement.

• HOW ARE PRIVACY AND CIVIL LIBERTIES SAFE-GUARDED?

Nominations to the Terrorist Screening Database are not accepted if they are based solely on race, ethnicity, national origin, religious affil-iation, or First Amendment–protected activities, such as free speech, the exercise of religion, freedom of the press, freedom of peaceful assembly, or petitioning the government for redress of grievances. In addition, Terrorist Screening Database nominations undergo several layers of quality assurance reviews and audits by nominating agen-cies, the National Counterterrorism Center or FBI (as appropriate), and the Terrorist Screening Center on a regular basis to ensure com-pliance with interagency standards. A dedicated privacy and civil liberties attorney at the Terrorist Screening Center supports this effort to confirm adherence to process and guidelines. The overall watchlisting and screening enterprise is also regularly reviewed by departments and agencies' Inspectors General, along with the U.S. Government Accountability Office. Lastly, the U.S. Congress pro-vides oversight through several of its committees.

• IF A PERSON HAS AN ADVERSE EXPERIENCE THAT THEY BELIEVE IS RELATED TO THE TERRORIST SCREENING DATABASE, HOW CAN THEY SEEK RECORDS CORRECTION? HOW CAN A PERSON

SEEK TO HAVE HIS OR HER NAME REMOVED FROM THE TERRORIST SCREENING DATABASE?

Anyone, regardless of citizenship, can contact the U.S. Department of Homeland Security Traveler Redress Inquiry Program (DHS TRIP) to resolve issues related to difficulties experienced during travel screening at transportation hubs, such as airports, seaports, train stations, or U.S. border crossings. This includes being delayed or denied boarding on an aircraft, or being identified for additional screening when entering or exiting the country

It may seem rather obvious, but known "terrorists" are on the gov-

Administered by the FBI, the Terrorist Screening Center (TSC) now provides "one-stop shopping" so that every government screener is using the same terrorist watchlist—whether it is an airport screener, an embassy official issuing visas overseas, or a state or local law enforcement officer on the street. The TSC allows government agencies to run name checks against the same comprehensive list with the most accurate, up-to-date information about known and suspected terrorists.

ernment's No-Fly List. Documents from the National Counterterrorism Center that were leaked to the press in 2014 show that the list includes people that have been convicted of or arrested for acts of terrorism, bombers, hostage takers, associates of terror groups, and assassins.

With those comforting facts in mind, these same documents show that federal agencies can nominate a person for that government blacklist if "an individual is known or suspected to be or has been knowingly engaged in conduct constituting, in preparation for, in aid of, or related to terrorism and/or terrorist activities."

Officially the Justice Department continues to say that any federal agency or governmental authorities must have *reasonable suspicion* that a person would actually pose a threat before they go onto any of the watch lists. However, the American Civil Liberties Union (ACLU) and many other civil rights/liberties activists group have argued that this reasonable suspicion is extremely subjective. Recent lawsuits that have gone all the way to the U.S. Supreme Court have ruled in favor of individuals placed on these lists with little or no explanations. However, many still believe that the system is still riddled with flaws.

You might end up on some of these governmental watchlists if you are a frequent traveler to known trouble spots. Countries that are known to be involved with terrorism, narcotics smuggling, and financial crimes can definitely raise red flags.

If you are a nonviolent political activist, you may also end up on the No-Fly or the heavily security-checked Selectee List. One documented case of an activist denied a boarding pass involved a former Princeton University professor who believes he was put on the list back in 2007 after giving a high-profile speech that was extremely critical of then-President Bush.

Another case took place in 2012 when Wade Hicks was stranded for a week in Hawaii while trying to travel back from a trip to Japan. Hicks was an organizer for the Tea Party in Mississippi and had been vocal about the importance of the U.S. Constitution, concern about high taxes, lack of transparency surrounding the 9/11 terrorist attacks, and government intrusions into people's private lives at political rallies and on a radio show he hosted called *Free Speech Zone.*

After being stranded on what should have been a simple layover while traveling back home, he was informed he was now on the No-Fly List. Hicks then contacted lawmakers in Mississippi and his story went viral with the press. There was even an article about his situation that appeared in a Russian newspaper! Soon after that, he received a telephone call from a U.S. customs agent telling him he had been had removed from the No-Fly List. There was no apology and no explanation for why he was put on the list or why he was suddenly now cleared to fly.

Another example for "no-fly" complaints can be as simple as having a name that is similar in sound or spelling to someone else who is on one or more governmental watchlists. Back in 2007, a group of people who were named Robert Johnson had numerous problems flying and traveling. It seems that a Robert Johnson had been convicted of plotting to bomb both a Hindu temple and a movie theater in Toronto, Canada.

A simple clerical error can also be the source of a no-fly nightmare. In 2004, a Stanford University student was placed on the No-Fly. It was not until 2011, and after numerous federal lawsuits, that it was determined that she was put on the list after an FBI agent had checked the wrong box on a form!

Some believe that individuals can and do end up on governmental watchlists, No-Fly Lists, and the Secondary Security Screening Selection Lists if they have outstanding warrants or pending criminal cases for completely unrelated matters. Civil right advocates say that this is unconstitutional, as people are innocent until proven guilty—not to mention that none of this has anything to do with aviation security.

The bottom line is that the curtain of secrecy that shrouds the No-Fly List still remains. The government maintains that secrecy about the No-Fly List is needed for maintaining national security. The logic is that a potential terrorist could be tipped off that the government is watching or investigating them if they were to receive a letter saying that they are on a watchlist or blacklist.

Recent high-profile Supreme Court rulings are supposed to make it easier for individuals to find out the reason they are on these watchlists, and the American Civil Liberties Union (ACLU) has been an active champion in assisting people who believed that they were wrongly placed on the No-Fly List and never offered adequate reasons from the government as to why. The ACLU's comprehensive guide to assisting American citizens that believe or know that they are on the U.S. No-Fly List is an excellent starting point for reading, understanding, and taking action to get their names removed. It is available at https://www.aclu.org/know-your-rights/what-do-if-you-think-youre-no-fly-list.

And while the airlines, federal agencies, and various governmental departments wrestle with who can and who cannot fly on commercial aircraft today, there are also large challenges and hurdles being faced with airport workers. In 2015, it was discovered that the Transportation Security Administration (TSA) had failed to identify seventy-three aviation employees with "active clearance badges" who had links to international terrorism! Directly affiliated with the passenger aircraft, these people included aircraft mechanics, onboard food-service and cleaning service workers, baggage handlers, and more.

A heavily edited thirty-four-page copy of the report from the Department of Homeland Security (DHS) was made public in June 2015, and was entitled "TSA Can Improve Aviation Worker Vetting." It can be found at https://www.oig.dhs.gov/assets /Mgmt/2015/OIG_15-98_Jun15.pdf.

The report says that the seventy-three employees of the major airlines, airport vendors, and other employees with terrorist ties had not been identified because the TSA was not authorized to receive all the terrorism-related information about these individuals because of "inter-agency policies"! The report recommended that TSA "request additional watchlist data, require that airports improve verification of applicants' right to work, revoke credentials when the right to work expires and improve the quality of the vetting data."

The TSA agreed with the recommendations.

And then in July 2015, another report from the TSA showed that undercover agents that tried to pass through security while carrying "fake prohibited items" were able to elude detection an alarming 96 percent of the time! Internal tests at almost all of America's busiest airports showed that TSA failed to find fake explosives and weapons in sixty-seven of seventy internal tests.

Most private aircraft and small charter planes are currently exempt from the security checks of flying on commercial airlines. Some are saying that this is a loophole that needs to be closed. People on the No-Fly List for airlines can and do rent or purchase planes for travel.

Improvements in airport security, passenger screening, airline-employee vetting, and even baggage handling are long overdue. Some regulations are lax and ludicrous, while others are borderline punitive and an infringement on personal civil rights. Unfortunately, there appears to be no quick fix or even long term resolutions or changes on the horizon. Many regular travelers believe that nothing much is going to change soon and are resolved to the idea that this is simply the way of the world and what everyone simply terms . . . *Welcome to travel in the twenty-first century.*

15

PROHIBITED ITEMS
FOR AIRLINE TRAVEL

If you are a regular traveler and have ever had to stand in a security line behind someone undergoing a thorough TSA search of carry-on luggage, you know how frustrating and time-consuming that process is! The bottom line is, you can't just pack your bags and purses the way you used to. Today, it really does help speed the security process by planning ahead and packing your carry-on and checked luggage properly.

Every traveler needs to know that there is a very long list of items that are prohibited from being brought on board a commercial airplane, and an equally long list of items that can only travel with you as checked baggage.

Show up with a screwdriver or even a wrench that measures less than seven inches in overall length, and you can breeze through security with your carry-on bags. Show up with a large jar of salsa or maple syrup, and your carry-on bag is going to be hand-searched and those "contraband items" are going to be confiscated if they are over 3.4 ounces!

Unfortunately, by the time you realize that you made a mistake, and your grandmother's jar of homemade gravy would have been fine in your checked bags, you will have to hand it over for confiscation (or finish it off before proceeding through security, depending on how good that gravy is!).

Also remember that the final decision rests with the TSA officer on whether an item is allowed through the security checkpoint.

If you are traveling with firearms, make sure that you check and double-check with the airline you are flying on for any additional restrictions that they may have. Some airlines today will not transport firearms as part of their corporate policies. Other airlines will transport them begrudgingly, but have everything from special transport requirements to additional fees.

The following list covers many of the "usual" items, as well as some of the "unusual" objects that the TSA has regulated or prohibited. There are also other hazardous materials that are regulated by the FAA. That information is summarized at www.faa.gov/Go/Packsafe.

> **R**—*Restricted—liquids less than 3.4 oz / 100 ml allowed.*
> **NO**—*Item is either prohibited, or has carry-on/checked luggage restrictions.*
> **YES**—*Item is cleared to take on airliner in either carry-on/ checked luggage.*

ITEM	CARRY-ON	CHECKED
Aerosols	R	NO
Aerosols are prohibited with the exception of personal care items or toiletries in limited quantities.		
Alcohol	R	YES
Ammunition	NO	YES
Check with your airline if ammunition permitted in checked luggage. Small arms ammunition for personal use must be securely packed in fiber, wood, or metal boxes or other packaging specifically designed to carry small amounts of ammunition. Ask about limitations or fees.		

ITEM	CARRY-ON	CHECKED
Axes and Hatchets	NO	YES
Baseball Bats	NO	YES
BB Guns	NO	YES
Billy Clubs	NO	YES
Blasting Caps	NO	NO
Bows and Arrows	NO	YES
Box Cutters	NO	YES
Brass Knuckles	NO	YES
Cattle Prods	NO	YES
Chlorine for Pools and Spas	NO	YES
Compressed Air Guns	NO	YES
Including paintball markers, may be carried in checked bagged without the compressed air cylinder attached.		
Creamy Dips and Spreads	R	YES
Cricket Bats	NO	YES
Crowbars	NO	YES
Disposable Razors	YES	YES
Drills and Drill Bits	NO	YES
Including cordless portable power drills.		
Dynamite	NO	NO
Electronic Cigarettes and Vaping Devices	YES	NO
The FAA prohibits these devices in checked baggage. Battery-powered E-cigarettes, vaporizers, vape pens, atomizers, and electronic nicotine delivery systems may only be carried in the aircraft cabin (in carry-on baggage or on your person). Check with your airline for additional restrictions. Remove all electronic cigarette and vaping devices from carry-on bags if checked at the gate or planeside.		
Fire Extinguishers and Other Compressed Gas Cylinders	NO	NO

ITEM	CARRY-ON	CHECKED
Firearms	NO	NO

Firearms carried as checked baggage MUST be unloaded, packed in a locked hard-sided container, and declared to the airline at check-in. The container must completely secure the firearm from being accessed. Locked cases that can be easily opened are not permitted. Be aware that the container the firearm was in when purchased may not adequately secure the firearm when it is transported in checked baggage. Only the passenger should retain the key or combination to the lock. Firearm parts, including magazines, clips, bolts and firing pins, are prohibited in carry-on baggage, but may be transported in checked baggage. Replica firearms, including firearm replicas that are toys, may be transported in checked baggage only. Rifle scopes are permitted in carry-on and checked baggage.

Contact the TSA Contact Center with questions you have regarding TSA firearm regulations and for clarification on what you may or may not transport in your carry-on or checked baggage.

ITEM	CARRY-ON	CHECKED
Fireworks	NO	NO
Flammable Liquid, Gel, or Aerosol Paint	NO	NO
Flammable Paints	NO	NO
Flare Guns	NO	YES

Flare guns may be carried as checked baggage but MUST be unloaded, packed in a locked hard-sided container, within hazardous material regulations, and declared to the airline at check-in.

ITEM	CARRY-ON	CHECKED
Flares	NO	NO
Fresh Whole Fruit	YES	YES
Fuels	NO	NO

Cooking fuels and any flammable liquid fuel is prohibited.

ITEM	CARRY-ON	CHECKED
Gas Torches	NO	NO
Gasoline	NO	NO
Gel-Type Candles	NO	YES
Golf Clubs	NO	YES
Gravy	R	YES
Gun Lighters	NO	NO
Gun Powder	NO	NO

Including black powder and percussion caps.

ITEM	CARRY-ON	CHECKED
Hammers	NO	YES
Hand Grenades	NO	NO
Hockey Sticks	NO	YES
Ice Axes/Ice Picks	NO	YES
Jam and Jelly	R	YES
Knives	R	YES
Except for plastic or round-bladed butter knives.		
Kubatons	NO	YES
A kubatons, or kuboton, is a self-defense weapon made of a hard-plastic body that measures around 5.5 inches in length, has a diameter of a thick marker pen, and attaches to a large keychain.		
Lacrosse Sticks	NO	YES
Lighter Fluid	NO	NO
Lighters	YES	NO
Lighters without fuel are permitted in checked-baggage. Lighters with fuel are prohibited in checked baggage, unless they adhere to the Department of Transportation exemption, which allows up to two fueled lighters if properly enclosed in a DOT approved case.		
Liquid Bleach	NO	NO
Maple Syrup	R	YES
Martial Arts Weapons	NO	YES
Meat Cleavers	NO	YES
Night Sticks	NO	YES
Non-Flammable Liquid, Gel, or Aerosol	R	YES
Up to 3.4 oz/100.55 ml or less that fits in one, clear, plastic, quart-sized resealable bag.		
Nunchucks	NO	YES
Oils and Vinegars	R	YES
Parts of Guns and Firearms	NO	YES
Pellet Guns	NO	YES
Pies and Cakes	YES	YES

ITEM	CARRY-ON	CHECKED
Pool Cues	NO	YES
Razor-Type Blades	NO	YES
Box cutters, razor blades not in a cartridge are prohibited in carry-on		
Realistic Replicas of Explosives	NO	NO
Realistic Replicas of Firearms	NO	YES
Realistic Replicas of Incendiaries	NO	NO
Recreational Oxygen	NO	NO
Non-medically required, flavored or canned oxygen containers are prohibited.		
Sabers	NO	YES
Safety Matches	YES	NO
One book of safety (non-strike anywhere) matches are permitted as carry-on items, but all matches are prohibited in checked baggage.		
Safety Razor with Blades (allowed without blade)	NO	YES
Salad Dressing	R	YES
Salsa and Sauces	R	YES
Saws	NO	YES
Including cordless portable power saws.		
Scissors	NO	YES
Metal with pointed tips and a blade length greater than four inches measured from the fulcrum are not allowed.		
Screwdrivers/Wrenches/Pliers	YES	YES
Less than seven inches in length.		
Self Defense Sprays	NO	YES
One 4 fl. Oz. (118 ml) container of mace or pepper spray is permitted in checked baggage provided it is equipped with a safety mechanism to prevent accidental discharge. Self-defense sprays containing more than 2 percent by mass of tear gas (CS or CN) are prohibited in checked baggage.		
Skates	YES	YES
Including ice skates and Rollerblades.		
Ski Poles	NO	YES

ITEM	CARRY-ON	CHECKED
Small Compressed Gas Cartridges	YES	YES

Up to two in life vests and two spares. The spares must accompany the personal flotation device and presented as one unit.

Soup	R	YES
Spear Guns	NO	YES
Spillable Batteries	NO	NO

Except those in wheelchairs. Spillable batteries are also known as wet cell batteries and are the type used in your car, truck, motorcycle, or boat.

Spray Paint	NO	NO
Starter Pistols	NO	YES

Can only be carried as checked baggage and *must* be unloaded, packed in a locked hard-sided container, and declared to the airline at check-in.

Strike-anywhere Matches	NO	NO
Stun Guns/Shocking Devices	NO	YES
Swords	NO	YES

Cutting or thrusting weapons, including fencing foils.

Tear Gas	NO	NO

Self-defense sprays containing more than 2 percent by mass of tear gas are prohibited in both carry-on and checked baggage.

Throwing Stars	NO	YES
Tools	NO	YES

Greater than seven inches in length.

Torch Lighters	NO	NO

Torch lighters create a thin, needle-like flame that is hotter (reaching 2,500 degrees F) and more intense than those from common lighters. Torch lighters are used for pipes and cigars, and maintain a consistent stream of air-propelled fire regardless of the angle in which they are held.

Turpentine and Paint Thinner	NO	NO
Vehicle Airbags	NO	NO
Yogurt	R	YES

16

TERRORIST GROUP PROFILES

The following is a list of some active terrorist organizations that continue to target innocent victims worldwide, as well as some of the more notorious and history-making groups from recent times. While your chances of being a victim of a terrorist attack are extremely low, common sense tells us all that while crossing a street it is wise to look both ways to avoid being hit by a car or a truck!

On the flip side, the chances of a traveler becoming a victim of a terrorist attack are still very real and growing. Rarely does a month or a week goes by in which a dastardly, cowardly, and deadly attack does not takes place somewhere in the world. The U.S. State Department reports on terrorism show that in 2015, there were 12,089 attacks, which resulted in the death of 29,376 innocent victims. While that number is down slightly from the year before, 2015 still rated as the second deadliest year on record.

Many hundreds of terror-oriented groups are known and being tracked internationally. Government anti-terrorist organizations and law enforcement groups worldwide continually struggle to stay up to date as new organizations are discovered and perpetrate their cowardly deeds. This list is compiled from various governmental and international sources. Some of the entries are less detailed than others, simply because less is known about some groups than others.

The U.S. Department of State maintains a list of nearly sixty terrorist groups and organizations on their website at http://www.state.gov/j/ct/rls/other/des/123085.htm, along with a listing of organizations that have been "de-listed" and are no longer considered active. The U.S. National Counterterrorism Center was established in 2004, and has the very comprehensive and easy to follow Terrorism Guide Website. This site (https://www.nctc.gov/site/index.html) contains many features across the full range of issues pertaining to international terrorism: terrorist groups, wanted terrorists, technical pages on various threat-related topics, and a historic timeline that marks dates that terrorists may believe are important if planning attacks to commemorate particular events.

Over the past decade, dozens if not hundreds of self-proclaimed terrorist groups and organizations have continued to spring up around the world. Some are little more than fronts and changed names for existing groups. This adds to the difficulty in being able to identify, track, and understand how many organizations are really out there and what their goals and objectives are.

Abu Nidal Organization (ANO) a.k.a. Fatah Revolutionary Council, Arab Revolutionary Brigades, Black September, and Revolutionary Organization of Socialist Muslims

Although the organization is now largely considered inactive, the group was an extremely active international terrorist organization in the 1970s and 1980s that carried out terrorist attacks in twenty countries that killed or injured almost nine hundred people. It demonstrated its ability to operate over wide areas, including the United States, Middle East, Asia, and Europe. Abu Nidal, founder of the group, was found dead in Iraq in August 2002. Whether he was assassinated or committed suicide is unclear. Current and former leaders and associates are now thought to be in Iraq, with cells in Palestinian refugee camps in Lebanon.

Abu Sayyaf Group (ASG)

The ASG is the most violent of the Islamic separatist groups operating in the Philippines. They have engaged in many kidnappings for ransom, bombings, assassinations, and acts of extortion. While it claims its motivation is to promote an independent Islamic state in the southern Philippines, many believe that it uses terror mainly for financial profit.

Afghan Taliban

With roots going back to the early 1990s, the word *Taliban* is Pashto for "students," and was composed of peasant farmers and men studying Islam in Afghan and Pakistani madrassas, or religious schools. In the years leading up to the September 11, 2001 attacks in the United States, the Taliban provided a safe haven for al-Qaida. This gave al-Qaida a base in which it could freely recruit, train, and deploy terrorists to other countries.

The Afghan Taliban are responsible for most of the insurgent attacks in Afghanistan. In January 2014, the group staged a suicide and small-arms attack on the popular Lebanese Taverna restaurant in Kabul, killing twenty-one people, including three Americans, marking one of the deadliest attacks against Western civilians in Kabul since 2001. In a one-week span in March 2014, the Taliban conducted four high-profile attacks in Kabul city, culminating in a March 28 attack on a heavily guarded guesthouse in Kabul for employees of a U.S. aid group. The targeted guesthouse was next to a Christian charity and daycare center that may have been the intended target. The next day, the Taliban conducted an attack on the headquarters of Afghanistan's election commission with rockets and automatic rifles, following an attack on the provincial election office earlier that week. On March 20 the Taliban attacked Kabul's luxurious Serena Hotel, killing nine civilians who were all shot at point-blank range by four insurgents who had smuggled in small pistols.

Al-Aqsa Martyrs' Brigade (AAMB)

The Brigade is made up of an unknown number of small cells of Fatah-affiliated activists at the start of the *intifadah* to attack Israeli targets. Its aim is to drive Israeli military and settlers from the West Bank, Gaza Strip, and Jerusalem to establish a Palestinian state. Shooting and suicide bombings are its hallmark, including claiming responsibility for the first suicide bombing carried out by a female.

Amnesty was offered to and later rejected by AAMB back in 2007. The group is still considered active today.

Al-Gama'a al-Islamiy ya (AGAI)

Egypt's largest militant group and active since the late 1970s. Known for armed attacks against Egyptian officials, Coptic Christians, and the spectacular November 1997 attack at Luxor that killed fifty-eight foreign tourists (sixty-two people in total). It has a worldwide presence, with members in the United Kingdom, Austria, Yemen, and Afghanistan. Some analysts speculate that AGAI was also involved in the assassination of President Anwar Sadat. AGAI has not carried out any terrorist attacks in almost twenty years, but is still considered active and dangerous.

Al-Nusrah Front

Al-Nusrah Front is one of the most capable al-Qaida-affiliated groups operating in Syria during their ongoing conflict. The group in January 2012 announced its intention to overthrow Syrian President Bashar al-Asad's regime, and since then has mounted hundreds of insurgent-style and suicide attacks against regime and security service targets across the country. The group is committed not only to ousting the regime, but also seeks to expand its reach regionally and globally

The group's cadre is predominately composed of Syrian nationals, many of whom are veterans of previous conflicts, including the Iraq war. Thousands of fighters from around the world have traveled to Syria since early 2012 to support oppositionist groups, and some fighters aspire to connect with al-Nusrah Front and other extremist groups. Several Westerners have joined al-Nusrah Front, including a few who have died in suicide operations. Western government officials have raised concerns that capable individuals with extremist contacts and battlefield experience could return to their home countries to commit violent acts. An al-Nusrah Front attack in May 2014—the first known suicide bombing by an American in Syria—targeted regime personnel, highlighting the involvement of U.S. persons in the conflict.

Al-Qaida

Founded by the most notorious terrorist of the twenty-first century, Usama Bin Ladin, the goal of al-Qaida is to establish a pan-Islamic domination throughout the world by working with allied Islamic extremist groups to overthrow regimes it deems "non-Islamic" and expelling Westerns and non-Muslims from Muslim countries. In a statement under the banner of "The World Islamic Front for Jihad Against the Jews and Crusaders," Usama said that it was the duty of all Muslims to kill U.S. citizens—civilian or military—and their allies everywhere.

Unfortunately for the world, the core of al-Qaida has dozens of affiliate and associated groups throughout the globe.

On September 11, 2001, a total of nineteen al-Qaida suicide attackers hijacked and crashed four U.S. commercial airliners—two into the World Trade Center, one into the Pentagon, and the fourth into a field in Pennsylvania—leaving about three thousand individuals dead or missing. Al-Qaida also takes credit for the attack on the USS *Cole* in 2000 that killed seventeen sailors, and bombings against U.S. embassies in Africa in 1998 that killed 301 individuals and injured more than five thousand civilians. Shoe bomber Richard Reid was an al-Qaida associate that was gang-tackled by passengers and stopped from igniting a bomb in his shoe on a 2001 transatlantic flight from Paris to Miami.

Two years after the horrific 9/11 attacks here in the United States, Khalid Shaykh Muhammad was arrested, charged, and convicted as the mastermind behind the plots that left 2,976 innocent victims killed in the World Trade Center in New York, at the Pentagon in Washington, and in the hijacking and crash of United Airlines Flight 93 in Pennsylvania. Muhammad is still a terrorist-guest at Guantanamo (GITMO) in Cuba and is facing the death penalty. Photo courtesy of NCTC.

The legacy of Osama bin Laden was one of blood, death, and attacks against many thousands of innocent people. The mastermind behind the 9/11 attacks and many others, the "world's most wanted terrorist" reign of hell came to an end in May 2011 when he was killed by U.S. special operations forces at his hideout in Pakistan. Photo courtesy of NCTC.

Al-Qaida is also the terrorist group responsible for the January 2015 attacks in Paris against the *Charlie Hebdo* newspaper and others related, where a total of sixteen people were killed and twenty-two were wounded.

Al-Qaida also had plans that were either thwarted or not carried out: assassinate Pope John Paul II, kill former President Bill Clinton, conduct midair bombings of a dozen U.S. trans-Pacific airliners, conduct underwear or shoe bombings of airplanes, and detonate bombs at Los Angeles International Airport.

Al-Qaida has hundreds of cells worldwide and terror experts continue to say it is not a question of *if* al-Qaida will attack again, but simply a question of *when*.

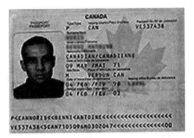

Ahmed Ressam, sentenced to twenty-two years in prison in 2005 for planning to bomb Los Angeles International Airport on December 31, 1999, acquired this ostensibly genuine Canadian passport by using a fraudulent baptismal certificate; the obscured name was Western-sounding in an attempt to evade scrutiny at the border. Photo courtesy of NCTC.

Al-Shabaab

Al-Shabaab has claimed responsibility for many bombings—including various types of suicide attacks—in Mogadishu and in central and northern Somalia, typically targeting Somali government officials, and the African Union Mission to Somalia (AMISOM). Since 2013, al-Shabaab has launched high-profile operations in neighboring countries, most notably the September 2013 Westgate Mall attack in Nairobi and the May 2014 attack against a restaurant in Djibouti popular with Westerners. The Westgate attack killed sixty-seven Kenyan and non-Kenyan nationals, and a siege continued at the mall for several days. In June 2014, an attack and siege in Mpeketoni, Kenya, killed nearly fifty tourists; although there was no claim of responsibility, al-Shabaab was widely believed responsible.

The al-Shabaab terrorist group operates in numerous countries in Africa. It is a radical Muslim extremist group that uses explosives, kidnapping, assassination, and extortion tactics. Its flag features an open copy of the Muslim Koran and two crossed AK-47 rifles.

Ansar Bayt al-Maqdis (ABM)

Ansar Bayt al-Maqdis (ABM) is the most active and capable terrorist group operating in Egypt. ABM shares al-Qaida's ideology and seeks the destruction of Israel, the establishment of an Islamic caliphate in the Sinai Peninsula, and the implementation of sharia law. The group is based in the Sinai but since the fall of 2013 it has expanded its operational reach into Egypt's Nile Valley.

ABM has not made explicit threats against the West or Western targets in its official propaganda. However, the group views the West, and the United States in particular, as supporters of Israel and Egypt and expresses anti-Western sentiment in its rhetoric.

Aum Supreme Truth (Aum) a.k.a. Aum Shinkikyo, Aleph

This cult established in 1987 aimed to take over Japan and then the world. Aum believes that the United States will initiate Armageddon by starting World War III with Japan. On March 20, 1995, Aum members simultaneously released the chemical nerve agent Sarin on several Tokyo subway trains that killed twelve people and injured nearly six thousand. Despite years of inactivity, the group remains under surveillance by Japanese authorities. Most of the Aum's 1,500 members live in Japan while about 300 are located in

While the world has yet to see a large-scale chemical or biological terrorist attack, experts believe that it is only going to be a matter of time until terrorists unleash this horror on innocent people. While chemical and bio weapons often require sophisticated factory and laboratories, many can be "brewed and concocted" with ingredients that are relatively easy to secure, especially on the worldwide black market.

Photo courtesy of NCTC.

Russia, says the State Department. The investigation of the 1995 attack remained cold until 2012 when three remaining fugitives were tracked down and arrested, finally closing the chapter on the worst terrorist attack in Japan's history.

Basque Fatherland and Liberty (ETA)

Primarily involved in bombings and assassinations of Spanish government officials, the ETA finances its activities through kidnappings, robberies, and extortion. Operating primarily in northern Spain and southwestern France, the group has killed more than eight hundred people, injured hundreds of others, and has carried out over 1,600 terrorist attacks.

A cease-fire that was negotiated in 2006 was broken in 2007, and since then ETA has continued to conduct frequent, low-intensity bombings throughout Spain.

Boko Haram

Formed in 2002, the group had alleged links to al-Qaeda, but in March 2015, the group announced its allegiance to the Islamic State of Iraq and Syria (ISIS). Since the current insurgency and attacks started in 2009, it has killed over 20,000 people, and displaced 2.3 million from their homes. Boko Haram was ranked as the world's deadliest terror group by the Global Terrorism Index in 2015, but has given up that dubious honor to ISIS for 2016.

This Nigerian terror group was already notorious for its acts of barbarism, but it grabbed world-wide headlines in April 2014 when members kidnapped 276 schoolgirls. Boko Haram, which loosely translates to *western education is sin*, continues to operate without much resistance.

HAMAS (Islamic Resistance Movement)

HAMAS has a goal of establishing an Islamic Palestinian state that would replace Israel. Article 6 of the group's 1988 Charter states that HAMAS "strives to raise the banner of Allah over every inch of Palestine and that Israel will exist only until Islam obliterates it." It has launched many attacks—including large-scale suicide bombings—against Israeli civilian and military targets. HAMAS has associations with other terrorist organizations, and leaders throughout the Middle East, including Syria, Lebanon, Saudi Arabia, and Iran.

Harakat ul-Mujahidin (HUM) a.k.a. Movement of Holy Warriors
The HUM is a militant Islamic group based in Pakistan that is linked to Usama Bin Ladin and al-Qaida. They use kidnapping, extortion, and murder frequently. Back in 1999 they hijacked an Indian airliner and are believed to have been involved and heavily responsible for the abduction and murder of U.S. journalist Daniel Pearl in 2001.

Hezbollah (Party of God) a.k.a. Islamic Jihad, Revolutionary Justice Organization, Organization of the Oppressed on Earth, and Islamic Jihad for the Liberation of Palestine.
This Lebanon-based radical Shia group and its splinter factions, takes its ideological inspiration and teachings from Iran's Ayatollah Khomeini. Its goal is the establishment of Islamic rule in Lebanon; the liberating of all occupied Arab lands, including Jerusalem and the elimination of Israel. It has been involved in numerous terrorist attacks against the United States, including the suicide truck bombings of the U.S. embassy and U.S. Marine Corps barracks in Beirut and numerous killings and kidnappings of U.S. and other Western hostages. Hezbollah has established terrorist cells in South America, Europe, Africa, and Asia.

IS, ISIS, or ISIL (Islamic State of Iraq and Syria)
Without question, IS, ISIS, or ISIL rates as one of the most brutal,

barbaric, and ruthless terrorist organizations of the modern twenty-first century. Effective, well-trained, and very adept at using all forms of social media, ISIS has become notorious for its videos of beheading of soldiers and innocent civilians, journalists, and just about anyone they deem a threat to their goals.

The international terrorist organization known as ISIS or ISIL funds itself and its followers by robbing, stealing, and selling antiquities and stolen oil throughout several countries in the Middle East. Several years ago, the organization was so emboldened as to announce to the world that it had developed its own currency, complete with gold coins.

They are a group of an estimated twenty thousand fighters and terrorists that are responsible for everything from mass murder, rape, slavery, and drug trafficking to suicide attacks on targets in Paris, France, and Brussels, Belgium.

In spite of being termed a "JV Team" (Junior Varsity) of terrorists, this fanatical Muslim army of psychos and zealots poses one

Terrorist organizations such as ISIS, al-Qaida, and others are using sophisticated press releases and booklets through the Internet to instruct sympathizers and potential terrorists on how to present themselves before attempting a terrorist attack. *The Safety and Security Guidelines for Lone Wolf Mujahideen and Small Cells* is a fifty-eight-page terror manual that was posted in English on several terror-related Internet websites and outlines how home-grown terrorists can carry out attacks without being noticed as a "Muslim."

of the greatest terrorist threats to everyone in the world. They continue to threaten direct attacks against the United States. Attacks such as the San Bernardino, California, Christmas party shooting, the attacks on the military recruiting office in Chattanooga, Tennessee, the shooting massacre at the nightclub in Orlando, Florida, and even the shooting in the baggage-claim area at the Fort Lauderdale, Florida, airport may have been ISIS motivated and inspired.

Islamic Movement of Uzbekistan (IMU)

The IMU's primary goal is the establishment of an Islamic state in Uzbekistan. Car bombings and kidnapping of foreigners—U.S. and Japanese citizens—are their hallmark. The IMU, in 2014, in conjunction with other militants, carried out an attack on Jinnah International Airport in Karachi, Pakistan, which killed thirty-six people, including the attackers, and wounded eighteen others.

They are believed to have associations with Taliban and al-Qaida terror groups, and in March 2015 leaders of IMU swore allegiance to ISIS. The militant terrorists are scattered throughout South Asia and have areas of operation in Afghanistan, Iran, Kyrgzstan, Pakistan, Tajikistan, and Uzbekistan.

Kurdistan Workers Party (PKK)

The PKK was founded as a Marxist-Leninist insurgent group primarily composed of Turkish Kurds with the original goal to establish an independent Kurdish state in southeastern Turkey. The organization now calls for autonomy for Kurds within Turkey, and seeks to promote the rights of Kurds living throughout Turkey. The group launched an armed struggle against Turkey in the mid-1980s, and has remained extremely active through the present day with kidnappings, car bombings, and explosives and firearm attacks.

Lashkar-e-Tayyiba (LT) a.k.a. Army of the Righteous

This group is one the largest and notorious groups in Pakistan and northern India that wants to liberate Kashmir and merge it with Pakistan using violent means. The group does not believe in attacking Muslims—but everyone else is fair game as victims!

LT has demonstrated their capabilities to carry out large-scale bombing attacks, armed assaults against civilians and military, and even a variety of maritime operations. In November 2008 they coordinated the bombing and shooting attacks on multiple targets across Mumbai city, including the Taj Mahal hotel. Ten gunmen with automatic weapons and grenades killed 166 people. Many were simply visiting tourists and travelers.

A candlelight vigil and memorial in 2008 for the many innocent victims of the terrorist attacks that took place in Mumbai, India.
Photo courtesy NCTC.

National Liberation Army (ELN)

The National Liberation Army, or ELN as it is known in Spanish, is the second-largest guerilla group operating in Colombia. Founded in the 1960s, ELN finances itself by kidnappings and through the lucrative cocaine trade. Their philosophy is a combination of communist ideology of Marxism and what is called "liberation theology."

Cease-fire talks to stop the violence against citizens and travelers have been an on-again, off-again proposition for over ten years, with new peace talks that started in the spring of 2016. If talks are successful, ELN will join the larger terrorist organization, the

Revolutionary Armed Forces of Columbia (FARC), in ending its fifty-year war. The peace treaty and disarmament process would bring all of Colombia's rebel-held territories back under government control.

Organization *al-Qaida* of in the Land of the Islamic Maghreb (AQIM)

Often shortened to *al-Qaida in the Islamic Maghreb* or AQIM, the group operates at this point primarily in North and West Africa regions. AQIM raises money through kidnapping for ransom and trafficking arms, vehicles, cigarettes, and persons, according to the U.S. State Department.

Since 2011, they have kidnapped and killed Western tourists and conducted suicide car bombings. In November 2015 they attacked a hotel in Mali where over one hundred travelers were taken hostage. The end result was that nineteen people were killed before security forces ended the siege. Thus far in 2016, AQIM has again attacked a hotel (126 hostages, 28 killed and 56 wounded), as well as attacking a town in the Ivory Coast that killed sixteen people, including four European tourists.

Revolutionary Armed Forces of Colombia (FARC)

Established in the mid-1960s as the military wing of the Colombian Communist Party, the FARC (Fuerzas Armadas Revolucionarias de Colombia) is Colombia's oldest, largest, most capable and best-equipped Marxist insurgency group. It has conducted bombings, murder, kidnapping, extortion, hijacking, as well as guerrilla and conventional military action against Colombian political military and economic targets. Foreign citizens and travelers have often been targets of the FARC kidnapping for ransom, as the group operated in many areas of Colombia, Venezuela, Panama, and Ecuador.

The Colombian government signed a final peace agreement on March 23, 2016, hopefully bringing an end to the longest civil war in Latin America. It is estimated that 225,000 people have been killed and six million displaced in the conflict. Only time will tell if the peace agreement holds, and the organization's terrorism comes to an end.

Revolutionary People's Liberation Party (DHKP/C) a.k.a. Dev Sol
The DHKP/C is a splinter faction of the Turkish People's Liberation Party/Front. It embraces a strong Marxist ideology and is virulently anti-U.S. and anti-NATO. Originally they targeted Turkish officials/diplomats, but over the years they have assassinated two U.S. defense contractors, wounded a U.S. Air Force officer to protest the Gulf War, fired rockets at U.S. consulates, and have conducted suicide bombings, targeting Turkish police.

CONCLUSION

If you haven't guessed that the days of carefree travel are over, you didn't really read through this book, and you are likely to end up making mistakes and creating danger for yourself, your family, and your friends that maybe could have been avoided. If, however, you realize that your safety and that of your travel companions is a responsibility that begins with *you,* chances are in your favor for years and years of safe domestic and international travel and adventures.

Staying informed, staying alert, and staying vigilant are a few of the keys to being able to travel safely and not be intimidated by the threat of terrorists or criminals.

The trends and statistics when it comes to terrorism—domestically and internationally—are not very encouraging. Even here in the United States there are no guarantees, quick fixes, magic solutions, safe-havens, or silver-bullet solutions to protecting ourselves from those who are crazed, criminals, or crusaders. Deranged individuals and groups detest and hate our freedoms, our morals, our great liberties, our autonomy, sovereignty, free will, and independence—and will continue to try to do us harm.

As Americans, we are blessed with great airline and travel opportunities to visit and enjoy destinations around the world. When travelers become frightened and cancel those visits because of terrorism in any region, the rogue terrorists actually WIN. They have taken away your right to travel freely. This is not to say that you should book your vacation to a known hotspot, but there are lots of precautions that any individual can take to make those travels much, much safer and secure.

Unregulated and unrestricted travel around our nation and around the world is but one of the many privileges that have been long guaranteed to everyone from our nation's early explorers and pioneers, to the modern business traveler, vacationer, and adventure seeker.

Giving up that right to free travel and transit allows those that are evil to win and hold all of us hostage. Let us hope and pray that day never comes.